PRAISE

CHURCH-PLANTING REVOLUTION

Winfield Bevins wants to start a revolution in church planting. He draws on his own experience as a church planter and lessons from a diversity of case studies. He covers a range of church-planting models and highlights universal principles every planter must wrestle with. He writes in a clear, engaging style. This book is ideal for those thinking about church planting, church planters, and their teams.

—STEVE ADDISON

AUTHOR OF *PIONEERING MOVEMENTS: LEADERSHIP THAT MULTIPLIES DISCIPLES AND CHURCHES*

Winfield Bevins is a fresh voice with new insights and solid church-planting experience. His insights are worth your time!

—ED STETZER

PRESIDENT, LIFEWAY RESEARCH

Church planting is one of the hardest and more rewarding things I have done in life. Bevins reminds us that the world needs more Christ-centered, disciple-making, Spirit-empowered, contextual churches, and that planting is one of the best ways to join God in his mission. Read this book and you might just find yourself planting a new church or helping to start one.

—JR WOODWARD

NATIONAL DIRECTOR, THE V3 MOVEMENT;
AUTHOR, *CREATING A MISSIONAL CULTURE*; AND CO-AUTHOR,
THE CHURCH AS MOVEMENT

The title itself is inviting. The content more than inviting. Winfield challenges us with his contention that church planting is one of the best ways to join God in his mission. His emphasis on contextualization and disciple-making, growing out of his own personal experience of planting, moves from the theoretical and adds needed relevance and integrity. I urge you to read it now and be challenged!

—MAXIE DUNNAM

AUTHOR AND FORMER PRESIDENT, ASBURY THEOLOGICAL SEMINARY

Church-Planting Revolution is exactly what we need—a succinct, straightforward, and compelling look at the necessity and hope of church planting. Winfield has given the body of Christ a great gift and I expect there will be many churches planted that would not have been, had it not been written.

—DR. CHRIS BACKERT
NATIONAL DIRECTOR, FRESH EXPRESSIONS US

Church-Planting Revolution is a clear and inspiring read for anyone interested in discovering how God is moving through church planting, and ultimately discerning how they might be involved. Winfield Bevins brings his rich and varied experience of personally planting a church, coaching church planters, and academic study to this dynamic resource.

—DREW STEADMAN
DIRECTOR OF U.S. CHURCH PLANTING, ANTIOCH MINISTRIES INTERNATIONAL

The twenty-first century demands a new and revitalized apostolic movement of disciple-making leadership like never before in the history of the church. *Church-Planting Revolution* give us just that! The church-planting principles offered in this book transcend cultures, languages, and context by interwebbing the DNA of movements with contemporary challenges for twenty-first-century America. As a national Hispanic missional leader, I have witnessed firsthand the heart of the author, but beyond anything his expertise, profound knowledge, and practical theology application for church planting and discipleship development for the transformation of the world.

—REV. DR. IOSMAR ALVAREZ
SENIOR PASTOR OF FUENTE DE AVIVAMIENTO AND
FOUNDER OF DISCIPLE 21 CHURCH PLANTING NETWORK

Winfield Bevins represents everything good and future-tense about global church planting. Having planted a church as well as a network, he is now in the business of raising up a whole new generation of planters to serve the global movement of God. With so much experience, one might expect a text with more lofty platitudes, principles, and plenty of success stories. Instead, Bevins offers the deeper, wiser perspective of a learner and kingdom servant, practically prescribing the shape of a planter's heart and soul. He wants to be where Jesus is working and he wants us to be there too.

—CAROLYN MOORE
FOUNDING AND LEAD PASTOR, MOSAIC UMC, EVANS, GEORGIA

Winfield Bevins calls himself "an accidental church planter," but there is no doubt that he is now both an experienced practitioner and a wise reflector of church-planting practice. This book is a gem—concise, digestible, and practical. It is at the top of my church-planting course booklist.

—RIC THORPE

BISHOP OF ISLINGTON, UK

Every era in the history of the church has both called for, and given us, the intelligent and anointed young minds required for the day. Winfield Bevins is a classic example. *Church-Planting Revolution* has a fresh, yet down-to-earth voice that adds richly to the conversation about church planting in the contemporary world.

—TODD HUNTER

BISHOP, CHURCHES FOR THE SAKE OF OTHERS AND
AUTHOR, *CHRISTIANITY BEYOND BELIEF*

This is a beautiful, simple little book for those considering church planting from ground zero and a perfect one for those mentoring new planters as they begin discernment. . . . Winfield Bevins brings all of himself as an inspiring kingdom thinker with connections to virtually every part of the North American church. A unique resource for what may be the most important movement of the church in our day: planting new congregations.

—GRAHAM SINGH

EXECUTIVE DIRECTOR, CHURCH PLANTING CANADA

I am thankful to my good friend Winfield Bevins for his passion to equip the next generation of church planters. This is a must-read for those who are exploring the call to church planting!

—WILL PLITT

EXECUTIVE DIRECTOR, CHRIST TOGETHER

This is the book so many in the church have been waiting for. This is a basic primer on church planting—a Church-Planting 101 guide—which dispels widespread myths about church planting and sets forth a practical how-to guide for aspiring church planters. This book is not only a gracious invitation, it is also a church-planting GPS, which will guide you to become part of the emerging church-planting movement sweeping the world. I heartily recommend it.

—DR. TIMOTHY C. TENNENT

PRESIDENT AND PROFESSOR OF WORLD CHRISTIANITY
ASBURY THEOLOGICAL SEMINARY

Dr. Bevins has put together something that is greatly needed: a simple and practical guide that does not make church planting the responsibility of ministry professionals alone, but brings it within the reach of the entire global church. He provides a clear pathway . . . with compelling and highly understandable prose, dialogical style, biblical content, and principle-based instruction. Church planting is firmly rooted in the Great Commission and is presented from a movement perspective. Potential church planters, both lay and theologically trained, will find a helpful apologetic to recruit others to this global cause. If you want to see many mobilized and pointed in the right direction, use this book!

—DR. GENE WILSON
CHURCH PLANTING CATALYST AND DIRECTOR, REACHGLOBAL AND COAUTHOR, *GLOBAL CHURCH PLANTING*

In a world of scholarly tomes and academic volumes, it is refreshing to read a primer on the subject of church planting. Dr. Winfield Bevins gives us concise biblical, historical, and field-tested wisdom around the art of planting new faith communities. This book will help awaken church leaders, lay persons, and clergy to the faith-filled possibilities and adventures of church planting.

—JORGE ACEVEDO
LEAD PASTOR, GRACE CHURCH, A MULTI-SITE UNITED METHODIST CONGREGATION CAPE CORAL, FORT MYERS, AND SARASOTA, FLORIDA

As a church planter and coach, I am frequently asked, "Where do I begin?" Now I have a great resource. *Church-Planting Revolution* captures the seminal thoughts, decisions, and practices that every would-be church planter must wrestle with. If church planting begins with a good foundation, this book is the first brick of that foundation.

—BRYAN D. COLLIER
FOUNDING AND LEAD PASTOR, THE ORCHARD, TUPELO, MISSISSIPPI

CHURCH

PLANTING

REVOLUTION

CHURCH

PLANTING

REVOLUTION

A Handbook for Explorers, Planters, and Their Teams

WINFIELD BEVINS

 Seedbed

Printed in the United States of America

Cover illustration and design by Strange Last Name
Page design by PerfecType, Nashville, Tennessee

Exponential is a growing movement of activists committed to the multiplication of new churches. Exponential Resources spotlights actionable principles, ideas, and solutions for the accelerated multiplication of healthy, reproducing faith communities. For more information, visit exponential.org.

Bevins, Winfield H.
    Church planting revolution : a handbook for explorers, planters, and their teams / by Winfield Bevins. – Frankin, Tennessee : Seedbed Publishing, ©2017.

        xviii, 127 ; 21 cm. + 1 videodisc

    Includes bibliographical references (pages 121-124).
    ISBN 9781628244588 (paperback : alk. paper)
    ISBN 9781628244625 (DVD)
    ISBN 9781628244595 (Mobi)
    ISBN 9781628244601 (ePub)
    ISBN 9781628244618 (uPDF)

    1. Church development, New--Handbooks, manuals, etc. 2. Church growth-- Handbooks, manuals, etc. 3. Discipling (Christianity)   I. Title.

BV652.24.B494 2017   283/.76713   2017950943

SEEDBED PUBLISHING
Franklin, Tennessee
seedbed.com

To Bill and Carol Latimer,
for your passion and commitment
to church planting

CONTENTS

FOREWORD

Responding to Peter's declaration that Christ was "the Son of the living God," Jesus proclaimed, "on this rock I will build my church, and the gates of hell shall not prevail against it" (Matt. 16:16–18 ESV). In that moment, the big fisherman's personal confession of faith, the rock of evangelism, became the foundation of the church. Let us always be clear, Christ alone builds the church; it is his own trophy of grace displaying the glory of his own holiness and power.

Introducing people to Jesus brings the church into existence and, apart from evangelism, the church would soon become extinct. That is why witnessing to the gospel is the first duty of every Christian. Yet turning to our Savior in repentance and faith is only the beginning of our response to the gospel. Certainly, we must be converted to enter "the kingdom of heaven" (Matt. 18:3 ESV). But the commission is to "make disciples," not converts (Matt. 28:19 ESV). A disciple is a learner or follower, as in the sense of an apprentice. Coming to Christ commits us to an ongoing process of learning, whereby we are progressively conformed to the image of our Lord. The objective is to disciple all nations, fulfilling God's command to our forebearers in the garden of Eden to be "fruitful and multiply and fill the earth" (Gen. 1:28 ESV). We live in one big world that God loves and for whom Jesus died and wants to reach through his disciples.

This quickly becomes evident at Pentecost when the Spirit-filled believers go out on the streets and begin to witness to the people from different nations gathered in Jerusalem (Acts 2). Then, prompted by persecution, Christians began to scatter to other cities, "preaching the word" wherever they went (Acts 8:4). Later, with the transformation of Paul, his missionary journeys spread the name of Jesus across the Roman Empire, establishing churches as he went. From these clusters of Christ followers, "the Lord's message rang out" to neighboring areas until their "faith in God [became] known everywhere" (1 Thess. 1:8 NIV)! What a beautiful explanation of how the church multiplies, ever expanding "to the end of the earth" (Acts 1:8)! Evangelism, discipleship, and church planting support each other, and when empowered by the Holy Spirit, nothing can keep the church from storming the gates of hell.

Bringing the message of redemption to every habitat of mankind underscores the urgency of world missions, but we must not limit the call to overseas workers. The missionary mandate flows out of God's love for the world. It is inherent in his very being, and every person born of the Spirit and incorporated into the body of Christ partakes in this nature. The most immediate and personal application of this truth comes out in our local churches and communities. Unreached people surround us, regardless of where we live. Many of them are lost, and likely have little regard for the church. Differences in culture, ethnicity, language, religion, and countless other disparities make communication difficult. Still Jesus loves all, and those in the household of God must keep seeking to build relationships and find ways to minister to the needs of all.

As we face the task presented before us by our Savior, we see that for our contemporary context, church planting offers one of the most effective ways of disciple making. While fresh to many, the concept of planting new churches is not a new idea. Actually, this practice goes back to the book of Acts, but in our present day, the church is rediscovering both the freedom and variety this discipline permits.

Winfield Bevins is on the forefront of this contemporary movement. He has studied the subject inside and out, traveling the world, observing different models of church plants, talking with their leaders, and sharing what he has learned as he goes. He gets right to the point, summing up practical lessons with deep simplicity. And before he finishes, you know how to take the first steps in planting a church.

What gives authenticity to his writing is his own experience as a planter. Bevins is a practitioner, not an armchair theologian. He does not claim to have all of the answers, but he has been around long enough to know most of the questions. We all can learn something from this man, and it is a pleasure to commend his teaching to you.

—DR. ROBERT COLEMAN
Distinguished Senior Professor of Discipleship and Evangelism
Gordon-Conwell Theological Seminary

ACKNOWLEDGMENTS

My church-planting journey has been influenced by many wonderful mentors and friends who have encouraged me along the way. In so many ways, they have helped inspire the content of this book. Therefore, I would like to thank several important people for helping make this book a reality.

First, I am thankful to my wife, Kay, and my three daughters, Elizabeth, Anna Belle, and Caroline, for joining with me in God's mission in church planting and for letting Daddy sneak away with his computer long enough to write this book.

I am thankful to the men and women of Church of the Outer Banks for letting me learn about church planting the hard way: by doing it!

I am especially thankful for the life and legacy of Dr. Robert Coleman. We built our church on the *Master Plan of Evangelism*. It is a great honor that he wrote the wonderful foreword to this book.

I am thankful to my friend Will Plitt, director of Christ Together Southeast, for his friendship and partnership in church planting over the last ten years. May God grant us many more years of working together for Christ!

I am thankful for my assistant, Ross Jenkins, who helped in so many ways with editing the manuscript. He is more than an assistant; he is a friend and brother.

I am thankful for J. D. Walt, Andy Miller, Mark Benjamin, and the rest of the wonderful team at Seedbed for helping me publish this book. I am honored to be a part of the Seedbed family of writers!

I am thankful for the amazing team at Asbury Seminary for our collaborative efforts to join together in God's mission to train a new generation of church planters!

I am thankful for Todd Wilson and Bill Couchenour at Exponential Resources for their partnership on this book and for their commitment to church multiplication.

Finally, I am thankful for the hundreds of men and women that I have taught and coached for planting new churches. I personally know the unique struggles, challenges, and joys of starting a new church. Church planters, you are my heroes and this book is written for you!

INTRODUCTION: JOIN THE REVOLUTION!

It's not just about one new church. It's about a whole new generation of churches.

—Steve Addison

As I am penning this book in 2017, I can't help but remind myself that this year marks the five hundredth anniversary of the Protestant Reformation. As we celebrate this monumental movement that has forever shaped Western culture, we are reminded of the power of people when they unite around a common cause. In the midst of our celebration and remembrance, if we simply look around, we will see that these types of movements aren't restricted to history books and past figures. As a matter of fact, we are living in an era of another, much quieter revolution. Whereas the Reformation focused much on doctrine, this new movement centers around the Holy Spirit as He calls His church back to the mission on which it was founded.

In *The Shaping of Things to Come*, Michael Frost and Alan Hirsch discuss this twenty-first-century movement wherein the church retreats from Christendom and attempts to recover the missional roots of the early church.[1] With the fall of Christendom—the name given to the church culture that has dominated European society from around the eleventh century until the end of the twentieth—the church no longer holds the prominent place in our culture that it once had.[2] The result of this drastic change in Western culture has been a major paradigm shift in the church's life. The church that could for so many years rely upon the culture of Christianity to ensure its existence is now beginning to reembrace mission as its primary focus.

Seeing the value of this missional impulse, a growing number of theologians and practitioners are encouraging the church to change its thinking so that it can make this missional shift. As this shift happens, Christians move from passive pew sitters to active missionaries in their communities who do not rely on formulas to grow the church. Instead, missional churches encourage their members to find ways to connect relationally with the people surrounding them. In *Breaking the Missional Code*, David Putman and Ed Stetzer explain how missional churches have broken away from the bonds of Christendom and have instead embraced the heart of the early church. According to Putman and Stetzer, these churches have done this by moving:

> From programs to processes
> From demographics to discernment
> From models to missions
> From attractional to incarnational
> From uniformity to diversity
> From professional to passionate
> From seating to sending
> From decisions to disciples
> From additional to exponential
> From monuments to movements[3]

What we are finding is this movement is only getting stronger. In fact, the missional shift is nothing short of revolutionary! From my perspective as a church-planting leader, I see the missional movement most clearly among my fellow comrades as they embark on the exciting, but daring venture of creating a new congregation. What I see is not a political revolution, but a spiritual revolution, where the Spirit is leading hundreds of women and men to join in God's mission to start new churches around the world.

For most people, the idea of church planting is revolutionary. Why? Because it shatters their paradigm of what it means to be the church. For most people, church is a building with a steeple and four walls. Church planting challenges this paradigm by calling us back to the New Testament, where the "church" meant a group of individuals who had come together in the name of Jesus Christ regardless of their building. The Greek word for "church" is *ecclesia*, which literally means "the called out ones," referring to the purpose of the people and not their location. Interestingly, the Oxford English dictionary describes "church" as, "A building used for public Christian worship." Over the ages, the concept of "church" has shifted from being a body to becoming a building. People have gotten it backward. Followers of Jesus must get back to an organic understanding of what it means to be the church, and church planting is a radical call back to the foundations of the church.

In many ways, church planting is like a new wineskin that reminds us that we aren't called to go to a church on Sunday morning, but that we are called to be a people on mission together in community. The old wineskins of Christendom can't hold the new wine of a church-planting revolution. Planting is radical because it takes individuals who are willing to join in God's mission and break free from old ways of being church and to break new ground with the gospel.

The fact that you are reading this book means you are interested in joining this church-planting revolution. However, you may be thinking to yourself, *Who? Me? I couldn't possibly imagine myself ever planting a church.* Well, you're not alone.

I myself am what you might call an "accidental church planter." I never planned on planting a church. My dream had always been to be a professor, but God had different plans for my life. In the spring of 2005, my wife and I felt the Lord calling us to start a new church. With nothing but a little faith, we began meeting in a home with only five people. After a few short months, we quickly outgrew the home meeting space, and the Lord opened a door for the church to meet at the local YMCA, which allowed us to continue to grow. After moving to the YMCA, the church grew to include people from all ages and backgrounds, many of whom had no church background at all. Over the next few years we witnessed dozens of people come to faith in Jesus Christ.

Many of the church members were surfers who had little or no church background at all. As a result, the church began to intentionally engage the surfing community and over time we reached dozens of surfers for Christ. Surfing is a communal sport and it became a wonderful way for us to build relationships with surfers and allowed us to share with them the love of Christ. I even learned how to surf and drove around with a surfboard strapped to the top of my car just in case there was a good wave. Several times a year, we would gather at the beach to perform ocean baptisms. After new believers were baptized we would give them an olive wood cross to commemorate their experience and entry into the community of faith. By embracing commonalities with the community around us, our church was able to establish deep connections with the unchurched and continuously reach out to those around us in a meaningful way.

Soon, we realized that God hadn't just called us to plant one church, but He was calling us to plant many other churches. Church planters began to come from all over to learn from what we were doing. Over time, God used us to help plant dozens of churches and to train hundreds of church planters across the nation. Little did I know, God was actually calling us to engage in a church-planting movement that spanned the entire globe.

Today, disciples of Christ across geographical boundaries, denominational lines, and cultural divides are planting new churches. Even as you are reading this, hundreds of new congregations are being started in order to make disciples in different communities around the world. This growth cannot be described as an isolated phenomenon. Rather, this is a movement of God. He is raising up a new generation of church planters who have a bold vision and a sincere passion to plant new churches to reach the world for Christ. Some are called to plant churches in cities, some in the suburbs, some in small towns, and others in out-of-the-way villages in remote parts of the world.

However, this movement is nowhere close to being completed. New churches are needed in every cultural, social, and economic setting. These churches are just waiting to be started by those who dare to step outside of the box and join with God as He enacts His mission in the world.

In the same way that the need for new churches is diverse in nature, church plants do not follow a single model. You will find traditional, multi-site, multicultural, urban, and house churches, and these only skim the surface of the spectrum. The reason we see such a variety is because one size does not fit all and one church cannot win all. Enacting the mission of God takes all kinds of churches to reach all kinds of people. It is important to match the model of planting with the culture, race, and ethnicity of the area in which you plan to plant a church.

We need to embrace and celebrate ethnic diversity when it comes to starting new churches. We need African Americans, Anglos, Asians, and Hispanics who are participating in planting new churches. In a similar way, we need diversity among various traditions, including Methodist, Presbyterian, Baptist, Anglican, Pentecostal, and Anabaptist, who are all planting new churches. Each group brings a different accent and flavor to the table to reach the harvest for Christ!

As for the personnel involved, once again, no one way is the correct way. For instance, some people choose to plant as a team, while others may choose to plant as a solo church planter. These factors are dictated by the setting of the envisioned church plant. God uses connections and regional factors to shape a vision for how the church should begin.

As with all churches, plants are simply a part of the larger global church. The global church needs new local churches to reach all types of people for Christ. In essence, the church mimics a mosaic or tapestry that consists of many colors. Each fragment displays a different color, but in unison, these individual pieces portray a beautiful masterpiece. Likewise, today there are many different expressions and types of church plants that are a part of the body of Christ.

Some new churches meet in buildings while others meet in homes. Some meet in bowling alleys, funeral homes, YMCAs, schools, and even outdoors under a tree. Some are traditional, some are contemporary, and some are home fellowships. In spite of the diversity, each new congregation of believers gathers as a local expression of being the global church wherever they are.

While church planting may be receiving more publicity now than in years past, it isn't a passing fad. The book of Acts, which in many ways is a church-planting manual, records the explosive growth of the early church through several key phases. This church-planting movement began in Jerusalem (see Acts 1–7), grew to Judea and Samaria (see Acts 8–12), and eventually expanded into the world (see Acts 13–28). The apostle Paul is one of the great examples of a pioneer church planter in the book of Acts, moving from city to city establishing churches among the Gentiles on his missionary journeys (see Acts 13–14; 15:40–18:22; and 18:23–21:17).

The pages of church history are full of amazing stories of men and women of faith who changed the course of history and influenced the world through church planting. Their stories remind us that the Lord can do extraordinary things through ordinary people who step out in faith to launch Christ-communities. Think about it for a moment. Every church that has ever existed underwent a stage of planting and infancy. Even though it might be hard to imagine, even your grandmother's church began as a plant! As you can see, joining in church planting isn't about beginning a revolution. Rather, it's about joining God's revolution as He brings reconciliation through the body of Christ.

ABOUT THE BOOK

This isn't a book about just starting one new church; it is about unleashing a movement of new churches. A few years ago I began dreaming of writing a short, simple book on church planting that would be highly practical and easy to use for a wide range of people. What you hold in your hands is a newly updated, revised, and expanded version of that dream. It is the fruit of more than a decade of church-planting experience and personal research. As I began putting words on the page, I saw myself speaking to three specific groups of people: explorers, planters, and team members.

> **Explorers**: Those of you who simply want to know what church planting is all about and how you might be a part of the process at some point in your life will find this book useful for self-discovery and exploring what church planting looks like. You will understand the whys and whats of starting a new church. The Church-Planting EQ assessment that I constructed in congruence with this book will be a supplemental resource to help you discern whether or not you are called to be a part of a church plant (see page 117).

> **Planters**: Those of you who feel the call to church planting and are beginning to explore where and how to start will see that this book will prompt you to ask the right questions and discern how to prepare a plant that fits your context. I will offer basic guidelines and models to develop a clear vision for your church. This book will prepare you for the initial strategic planning phases of church planting.

> **Teams:** Those of you who are following the call of God by joining a team will find this book a great resource to build a mental and spiritual picture of what a church plant could be. You may be a volunteer or a paid staff member, but regardless of your status, it is important that you formulate how you best fit into the overall mission of the church.

This updated version includes several new chapters, as well as a number of tools and resources in the appendices of the book. I have structured the new version in a way that can be easily used in a handbook format for church planters and their team members. The goal of this new edition is to be a resource that will guide you to think, dream, and plan as you walk through the entire process of planting and multiplying new churches from conception to birth.

SPECIAL FEATURES OF THE BOOK

> **Reflection Questions.** At the conclusion of each chapter, I have included questions that will help guide you to think through the ideas of this book and to implement them in your own context. The book can be used as a discussion guide for individuals, church-planting teams, leadership training, or as a small-group resource.

> **Church Plant Profiles.** Throughout the book you will also meet a variety of church planters from different contexts and hear their stories. My hope is that their stories will inspire you to envision how the Lord might use you to start a new contextualized church.

> **EQ Assessment.** In the back of the book you will be given free access to the Church-Planting EQ Assessment. The assessment gives a snapshot of your life and ministry experiences in order to discover your readiness for church planting. While there are no magical assessments that guarantee success, this guide is intended to be an initial self-assessment tool that will help you gain a more well-rounded under-standing of your potential calling to the ministry of church planting.

> **Strategic Plan.** Every new church should start with a detailed, written strategic plan to guide them through the process of church planting. The back of the book

includes an outline for a written church-planting strategic plan that can assist you and your church-planting team.

> **Demographic Worksheet.** Getting to know your context of ministry is an essential part of strategic planning for church planting. The book also includes a demographic worksheet to use as you collect information about the people living in your target area.

> **Action Items.** Each chapter includes several key action items to encourage you to fully engage with the content of the book. These action items will make what you are reading come alive as you encounter the realities of starting a new church for yourself or as a team.

Finally, this book is not about a model or program. God does not make robots. He is not a cookie-cutter God. Regardless of whether you are in a city, in a rural community, or on an island, this book will outline general principles that will help you develop a unique church-planting process that fits your context. As you and your church-planting team set out to plant a church, start with the transforming love of Jesus Christ as your foundation and then let people grow naturally. It's been famously said that every journey begins with the first step, so I invite you to begin the journey of joining the church-planting revolution by starting a new church wherever you stand today.

CHURCH PLANT PROFILE

Planter: **Matt LeRoy**
Type: **Missional**
Church: **Love Chapel Hill**
Location: **Chapel Hill, NC**

In the heart of Chapel Hill, North Carolina, is a new church that is reaching a diverse group of people with the love of Jesus. While Matt LeRoy was attending Asbury Seminary, God called him to return to his hometown of Chapel Hill to plant a new kind of church. Each week, the church holds two services in a local theater on Franklin Street in downtown Chapel Hill. The church has grown to an average of two hundred weekly; however, they have a wider community impact beyond their Sunday-morning attendance.

Matt said, "Our name is our mission. We want to love Chapel Hill with the heart of Jesus."[1] Love Chapel Hill encourages its congregation to love local, whether sharing a meal with someone in need, volunteering as a tutor, giving hot chocolate to students on exam days, or paying for parking on one of the busiest streets. To those serving at Love Chapel

Hill, these actions are more than random acts of kindness. To accomplish their mission, the church also partners with various community outreaches to fulfill their mission of loving Chapel Hill. Some of these include Grace on Wheels that provides transportation to those in poverty, SECU Family Housing that uses volunteers to feed and house families with loved ones in the hospital, or TABLE that feeds children with food insecurities in the community.

Often church plants focus on families or one particular group of people; however Love Chapel Hill is unique in that it doesn't have a target audience. Instead, it seeks to impact the entire community of Chapel Hill. Historically, those with bright futures don't mix with those with broken pasts. Yet, in this church, those differences are pushed aside. Love Chapel Hill is an eclectic mix of college students, young families, and those experiencing homelessness.

During the first service, Matt remembers two people on opposite ends of the socioeconomic spectrum sitting near the front of the church, with a few seats separating them. One was a well-dressed college girl. The other was a homeless man. As Matt asked the congregation to turn to a particular passage of Scripture, the college student moved to sit next to and share her Bible with the homeless man who didn't have one. "This was the first service, and that's when it clicked that that's what we're here for, and that's what we're going to do," Matt said. "We don't have a homeless ministry or a college ministry. We have a church family, and all of us are a part of that together."[2] Matt LeRoy and Love Chapel Hill are a wonderful example of a new church that is focused on trans-forming their community with the love and message of Jesus. For more information about Matt and Love Chapel Hill, visit **http://asburyseminary.edu/voices/matt-leroy**.

CHAPTER ONE

WHY START NEW CHURCHES?

We need new practices of church planting for the challenges of a post-Christian society.
—David Fitch

Maybe you are thinking, *Why do we need to start new churches? Aren't there enough churches already out there?* In this chapter I want to discuss why we need new churches and try to answer some of the major myths about church planting. As we scan the pages of Scripture and also our surrounding world, we see that the world is in desperate need of new churches.

One of the major reasons for planting new churches finds its foundation in the narrative story of Scripture. The story of creation portrays the God of Abraham, Isaac, and Jacob as one who pursues reconciliation with His creation, and His chief instrument for conducting His mission of reconciliation is the person of Jesus Christ. As we study the life of Christ, we see that He was from the Father and that He focused on training others to carry out the mission of the Father. In His own words, Jesus proclaims, "As You sent Me into the world, I also have sent them into the world" (John 17:18). Being that Christ is the head of the church and the church is the body of Christ, church planting is our response to the sending commission of Jesus.

> Jesus, undeterred, went right ahead and gave his charge: "God authorized and commanded me to commission you: Go out and train everyone you meet, far and near, in this way of life, marking them by baptism in the threefold name: Father, Son, and Holy Spirit. Then instruct them in the practice of all I have commanded you. I'll be with you as you do this, day after day after day, right up to the end of the age." (Matt. 28:19–20 THE MESSAGE)

Many Christians and churches teach that missions are something we support or do, such as sending or supporting missionaries in other countries. This may have been the case twenty to thirty years ago, but in the twenty-first century, the mission field has come to us. We live in a post-Christian world where people simply don't know the gospel anymore. Therefore, we are all called to be missional and share in the mission of God. Ed Stetzer wrote, "Missional means actually doing mission right where you are. Missional means adopting the posture of a missionary, learning and adapting to the culture around you while remaining biblically sound."[3]

The missional heart of God is the basis for church planting. God is a sending God who compels us to join Him in mission. According to missiologist Christopher Wright,

> Mission belongs to our God. *Mission is not ours; mission is God's.* . . . it is not so much the case that God has a mission for his church in the world but that God has

a church for his mission in the world. Mission was not made for the church; the church was made for mission—God's mission.[4]

Thus being missional isn't about creating something from nothing. Rather, it is about joining a mission that has existed from the beginning of time. British church planter Tim Chester reminds us, "Church planting puts mission at the heart of the church and church at the heart of mission."[5]

While we see that church planting is joining in God's narrative of history, we also know that church planting serves this mission through practical means. Roughly one-third of the people on the planet are still without a local church. The need for planting churches in global urban centers and among unreached peoples is growing daily because more than two billion people who have never heard of Jesus now inhabit our planet. That equals 6,500 unreached people groups who are waiting to hear what God has done for them.[6] Many of these lesser-reached peoples are from restricted-access countries and locations resistant to the Christian message. In order to reach these people, we must provide Christ-communities in which they can interact and grow spiritually as the body of Christ. In the words of John Stott, "We must be global Christians with a global vision because our God is a global God."[7]

Yet as we speak of the global proportions of unreached persons, all we have to do is look in our own territory and we can see the epidemic. For those of us who live in North America and Europe, we see a growing number of people all around us who are radically unchurched or, as Professor Alvin Reid defined, "those who have no clear personal understanding of the message of the gospel, and who have had little or no contact with a Bible-teaching, Christ-honoring church."[8] In the United States alone, there are 180 million people who have no connection to a local church, making it the largest mission field in the Western Hemisphere and the third largest mission field on Earth.[9]

The world is experiencing a major paradigm shift from modernity to postmodernism. The postmodern paradigm shift can be compared to previous time periods such as the Reformation or the Age of Reason. Leonard Sweet says, "The seismic events that have happened in the aftermath of the postmodern earthquake have generated tidal waves that have created a whole new world."[10] The changes of postmodernism have created a new world of postmodernity. Millard Erickson says that postmodernism is based on the following categories:

> The denial of personal objectivity
> The uncertainty of knowledge
> The death of any all-inclusive explanation
> The denial of the inherent goodness of knowledge
> The rejection of progress
> The supremacy of community-based knowledge
> The disbelief in the objective inquiry[11]

The changes of the postmodern world are real, but the church has been slow to address them. Too often, the church has been one of the last institutions to acknowledge and engage contemporary thought and culture, and many churches have chosen to respond to the changes in our culture with apathy and denial. It's no wonder that an estimated three to four thousand churches close every year.

How will we reach these people with the gospel of Christ? Experts agree that culturally relevant church planting is one of the most effective ways to reach unchurched people and make new disciples for Jesus Christ. Professor C. Peter Wagner went as far as to say that planting new churches is "*the* single most effective evangelistic methodology under heaven"[12] (emphasis mine). Likewise, statistics show that it is much harder for traditional churches to reach the unchurched. Therefore, there is an even greater need to plant churches that reach the unchurched for Jesus Christ.

I have seen that church planting is an effective way to reach unchurched people firsthand. Let me tell you Adam's story. Adam was the first person who came to faith in our new church. He was a young schoolteacher who did not grow up going to church. The few times that he did attend a church, he was exposed to bad church politics, and so he came to believe that most Christians were hypocrites. Sadly, he was exposed to religion—not to a relationship with Jesus—and he wanted nothing to do with church.

Adam always considered himself a good guy who never really did anything bad. Then he and his wife attended our first Christmas service at our new church. That morning I was preaching a sermon called "From the Cradle to the Cross" on the significance of the birth of Jesus. At the conclusion, I invited everyone to respond to the message by accepting Jesus into his or her heart. That day Adam gave his heart to Jesus Christ, and his life was forever changed. Over the course of the next five years, Adam's entire family came to faith, including his mother, father, and sister! Today he is still walking with Jesus, and he is an important leader in our church.

SIX COMMON MYTHS OF CHURCH PLANTING

Now that we have seen the necessity for church planting, I want to address a few of the myths against such a movement. After conducting a series of interviews with a variety of people, I have compiled a list of six common myths that surround church planting. In an effort to help newcomers understand the reality of church planting, I have listed fact-based responses to each of these six myths.

1. TOO MANY CHURCHES ALREADY EXIST

Reality: As we have already said, there are two billion people who do not know Jesus, and nearly one-third of the people on the planet do not have a local church to attend. The truth is, despite how many churches you see in your community, the vast majority of people around the world are not connected to a local church. Consider the following statistics in North America alone.

> In 1900, there were twenty-eight churches for every 10,000 Americans.
> In 1950, there were seventeen churches for every 10,000 Americans.
> In 2000, there were twelve churches for every 10,000 Americans.
> In 2011, the latest year available, there were eleven churches for every 10,000 Americans.[13]

The fact is, many denominations in North America are declining rather than growing while the population has more than quadrupled! Eighty to 85 percent of all churches in the United States have either stopped growing or are in decline, and an estimated three to four thousand churches close their doors each year![14] Only 17.5 percent of the population is attending a Christian church on any given weekend and that figure is projected to fall to 14.7 percent by 2020.[15] So how can we combat this drastic decline? The answer is that we need new churches that are planted according to a scriptural model to reach people with the gospel of Jesus Christ! Ed Stetzer and Daniel Im remind us, "Church planting is essential. Without it Christianity will continue to decline in North America."[16]

2. PLANTING NEW CHURCHES WILL HURT EXISTING CHURCHES

Reality: Becoming involved with church planting can actually bring new life and missional vitality to existing churches, pastors, and church members. Church planting isn't just for lone-ranger church planters, but works best if it is in concert with existing congregations working together to expand the kingdom of God through starting new churches in a city or region. Churches that engage with church planting can be energized and experience new life as they seek to recover the mission of God in their community or region. British church planters Tim Chester and Steve Timmis believe that existing churches can benefit from partnering with new ones, "Far from weakening a sending church, church planting is a vital opportunity to refocus the life of the church on the gospel."[17]

The important thing to take into consideration is communication among local churches and pastors. Oftentimes, church planters don't seek the support of local churches and come across as if they are trying to do their own thing. I would recommend that you avoid this at all cost. Also, if you are a pastor or a member of a local church, I would encourage you to find ways that your church can help be involved in church planting. It might just bring new life to your church!

3. CHURCH PLANTING IS TOO EXPENSIVE

Reality: Church planting doesn't have to be expensive. Congregations can meet in homes, coffeehouses, or other locations that do not require a lot of start-up money. If you are talking about raising money for a full-time salary for multiple staff, buying a building, etc., then you are right. There are only a few who can pull off that type of church planting prior to starting a new church. However, many people are able to start a new church on little to nothing.

Church leaders like Neil Cole, who oversees Church Multiplication Associates, advocates an organic approach to church planting that is small and focused primarily on discipleship.[18] These churches are finding unique ways to make disciples that do not require the expenses of traditional church buildings, structures, and staff salaries. Likewise, fresh expressions of church are an inexpensive alternative to expensive traditional models of church planting. My friend Shawn is effectively planting fresh expressions of church among his fellow restaurant workers with little to no start-up money.

4. CHURCH PLANTING IS ONLY FOR A SELECT FEW

Reality: Church planting offers a place for everyone to get involved regardless of age, background, nationality, race, or gender. It takes all kinds of people to be involved with starting new churches. It will take all kinds of churches and all kinds of people to reach all kinds of people. Men, women, children, families, the young, the elderly—church planting is for everybody! While everyone is not called to be the lead church planter, I do believe that everybody can be involved in church planting in a variety of ways, which we will discuss later on in this book.

Also, church planting isn't just for young people. Nothing could be further from the truth when it comes to church planting! Church planting is one of the most multigenerational ministries that I have witnessed. People who are involved in church plants are from all ages and backgrounds. When I was working on my doctorate, a fellow student named Bill who was in his seventies had planted a church in a retirement community in Florida. In a few years, the church that Bill planted had grown to more than one thousand members. I want to be like him when I grow up!

5. CHURCH PLANTING IS WHAT MISSIONARIES DO, OVER THERE

Reality: In many ways, North America has become the new mission field. Whether you like it or not, the mission field has come to you, regardless of where you live. I strongly believe that church planters are modern-day missionaries serving in a variety of new mission contexts. Church planting is needed in every context, in every part of the world. There are new churches being planted in all parts of the world, including rural, suburban, urban, and even mall churches, to name a few.

We need churches to be planted in every city, region, and nation to reach the two billion people globally who do not know Jesus Christ. Church planters are always looking for where they can start a new church. As I drive around a new city I often find myself thinking, *That would be a great place to start a new church.* As you look around, begin to think like a missionary and assess the needs of your city. Ask yourself the question, "Where does my community need a new church?"

6. A CHURCH PLANTER NEEDS TO BE AN EXTREME EXTROVERT

Reality: There is a common stereotype that church planters are type A, extroverted, caffeinated, charismatic individuals who can draw a big crowd, but I would strongly challenge that notion. This myth has kept more people from engaging in church planting than any other. The truth is, God uses all kinds of people to plant all kinds of churches.

Many of the church planters I have met are not extreme extroverts, but ones who share a common passion to reach beyond themselves to see people come to Christ through planting new churches. While church planting does involve trying new things and being flexible, it does not require that you be an extreme extrovert. A friend of mine named Ben was turned down by a church-planting network for not being an extrovert. I began to coach him and he eventually planted a church that grew to more than five hundred people and became a regional network leader. The work of church planting calls for someone who has a humble heart and is willing to do whatever the Lord has called them to do.

As we can see, many of the common myths about church planting are not accurate, nor do they give a reasonable excuse for us not to plant new churches. The mission of God and the sheer number of unchurched people in the world compel us to plant new churches in every context. To me, the real question is not "Why should we plant new churches?" but "Why should we *not* plant new churches?!" Church planting is not an option for Christians, but a call to fulfill the Great Commission of making disciples throughout the world. Now that we have explored the need for church planting and overcome some of the common myths and stereotypes, we can begin to lay the foundations of church planting.

ESSENTIAL THOUGHT

God's movement through history, and the two billion souls in need of the gospel, compel us to engage in church planting.

DISCUSSION QUESTIONS

1 What are the two major reasons presented in this chapter for starting new churches?

2 Do you agree with the reasons the author mentioned for church planting? Why?

3 Are there additional reasons you think we should plant new churches? If so, take a few minutes to discuss them.

4 Where are some areas of the world or cities that you think need a new church? Discuss where and why.

5 What are some of the reasons that you think it is necessary to plant a new church in your context?

ACTION ITEMS

Walk/drive around the city, town, or community where you are thinking about starting a new church. Identify what parts of the community might need a new church most.

Use the demographic worksheet in the back of the book to help you assess the people and needs of your city or community.

CHURCH PLANT PROFILE

Planters: **Pete and Bee Hughes**
Type: **Mother-Daughter**
Church: **KXC**
Location: **Kings Cross, London, England**

KXC is a church plant in the heart of London that was planted out of St. Mary's Bryanston Square on February 14, 2010, by Pete and Bee Hughes. The couple "were sent out from St. Mary's with a small group of leaders and a simple vision: to recklessly give themselves away to God, each other, and the people of King's Cross and beyond."[1] They are also a part of the HTB (Holy Trinity Brompton) Church-Planting Network, which is a church-planting movement within the Church of England.

KXC began meeting for Sunday gatherings at the Lumen United Reform Church and currently meets in the Ethiopian Church on Pentonville Road. Throughout the week they gather in homes and pubs, and other spaces around the King's Cross area, and through their outreach, the congregation has grown to become an eclectic mix of several hundred young adults, students, and young families. According to their website:

> [W]e've welcomed in new students and graduates arriving in London; we've welcomed people that had

*given up on God and church but have since redis-
covered faith and community; and we've welcomed
people who have no faith in Jesus, but just enjoy
coming along. Some of those have since found faith
in Jesus, others haven't, but wherever people have
come from, it's been a privilege to welcome them into
the community and to all that God is doing in and
through the church.*[2]

KXC has a bold vision to reach their part of the city
of London with the message of Jesus through kingdom
partnerships.

*In many ways the KXC adventure has been a story of
God building his church, as he promised, and being
incredibly faithful as we've sought to be obedient and
keep in step with him. We've seen God move in amazing
ways: in other churches generously allowing us to rent
their buildings at an affordable rate, local businesses
giving us rent-free office space, stories of God providing
homes for people to move into the area, and financial
provision out of nowhere in times of uncertainty. We've
seen people come to faith, return to faith, and grow in
faith. And whilst we celebrate all of the above, we do so
in the firm belief, that whilst Christ remains head of this
church, the best at KXC is yet to come.*[3]

KXC is a wonderful example of how God uses kingdom
collaboration to give birth to new contextualized churches in
England. For more information on Pete and Bee Hughes and
KXC, visit **http://kxc.org.uk**.

CHAPTER TWO

LAYING THE FOUNDATIONS

Church planting involves laying foundations.
—Stuart Murray

As we begin to formulate the vision of a specific church plant, it is important to establish a definition of what exactly is church planting. For this book, I define church planting as *joining in God's mission to plant and multiply disciple-making churches in every context.* Let me unpack this definition. First, church planting is joining in God's mission to redeem the world. In other words, the work of starting a new church begins with God and not with us. Too often we can think about church planting as our work, but in fact, when we plant, we join in the work God is already doing. As we have already seen in chapter 1, God's mission is the very foundation of church planting.

Second, at the heart of church planting lies the work of discipleship. Church planting is a natural outgrowth of answering Jesus' call to "come . . . and follow Me" (Mark 8:34; 10:21; Luke 9:23; 18:22) and "go therefore and make disciples" (Matt. 28:19). In other words, it's all about making disciples in every home, every town, every city, and every nation. Church planting is simply a contextual model of answering the call of Christ to go and make disciples. Discipleship is not a program that has a beginning and an ending point. Rather, it is an ongoing process that is dynamic and organic in nature. In the words of Ed Stetzer, "Discipleship is not just a course or series of studies. Discipleship begins with conversion and continues as an ongoing process. 'Make disciples' means that the church is to win people to Christ and grow these new converts in the faith. That process is meant to take place in the local church."[4] Therefore, the call of discipleship is an absolute essential to the work of church planting.

Third, when talking about church planting, it is important to note that we are talking about planting "churches." A church is not a building or a non-profit community organization. The church is a body of believers who have been called out by Jesus to be His body in heaven and on earth. At its most basic level, the church is the body of Jesus Christ. There is only one true church, and it is made up of all true believers in Jesus Christ. The apostle Paul reminds us, "Just as a body, though one, has many parts, but all its many parts form one body, so it is with Christ. . . . Even so the body is not made up of one part but of many" (1 Cor. 12:12–14 NIV). Just as the physical body has to have a structure to hold it together while allowing it to grow and develop, the body of Christ has an organic structure where each member has a role to play. If one member of the body is out of place or is not working, the rest of the body suffers as a result (see 1 Corinthians 12:26).

Fourth, we are talking about planting new, contextualized churches. Today there are many different expressions of the local church, which represent the body of Christ in a variety of contexts. The church in Africa looks different than the church in Texas; each one is called to be the church in its unique context and culture. In *Church for Every Context,* Michael Moynagh praises contextualized church for being able to "seek to fit the culture of the people they serve."[5] Over the last few years I have been able to experience many new contextualized churches around the world in cities, in jungles, and on the top of mountains. Each church was a little different; however, they all had one thing in common: they were all members of the body of Jesus Christ. These experiences have profoundly shaped my vision of church planting.

As we progress into defining a church based on its discipleship intentions, I want to dissect what I think is an excellent working definition of church planting provided by Professor Aubrey Malphurs. He wrote, "I define church planting as an exhausting but exciting venture of faith, the planned process of starting and growing local churches based on Jesus' promise to build his church and in obedience to his Great Commission."[6] Based on the pillars of this model, church planting is:

EXHAUSTING

Be forewarned: church planting is not for the faint of heart. It is exhausting and will require a radical commitment to the work. The road to church planting is littered with pastors who have burned out, committed moral failure, or simply walked away from the ministry. For many, what started out as an exciting adventure ended up as a nightmare. Therefore, I encourage everyone who is thinking and praying about church planting to count the cost and to know that it will be hard work.

Know that church planting will be challenging to your family, finances, and faith. At the same time, not all church-planting ventures end in disaster, failure, or frustration. Many church planters can and do thrive in various contexts, but it is still important to do your homework and know the facts about church planting before you begin.

A VENTURE OF FAITH

Church planting is not just a good idea; it is a work of faith from beginning to end. Church planting is an entrepreneurial endeavor that involves starting something from nothing, but the success is firmly rooted in God's grace rather than in human efforts alone (see 1 Corinthians 3:6). Planting begins with a seed of faith that must be grown and involves hard work and prayer to do the impossible of starting a new church.

We can't build a church on our own strength or merit; it is a work of grace from beginning to end. In the great faith chapter of the Bible, we are told that "without faith it is impossible to please Him, for he who comes to God must believe that He is, and that He is a rewarder of those who diligently seek Him" (Heb. 11:6). The Lord promises to respond to our prayer of faith. If you are considering starting a new church, ask the Lord to give you a bold faith for the work.

A PLANNED PROCESS

While church planting is organic, it will require a lot of planning and preparation. In other words, church planting doesn't just happen; it is a deliberate and intentional planned process. For some reason, certain people think that planning is unspiritual. Nothing could be further from the truth. In the words of Habakkuk, "Write the vision; make it plain on tablets, so he may run who reads it" (Hab. 2:2 ESV).

Developing a church-planting plan will help others join in what God is calling you to do. It will let people know the facts about how they can help. I have learned that people want to help if they are properly informed, so communication is the key. You will be amazed how willing people are to join the cause of church planting if they know the "what" and "why." Developing a plan will help you accomplish this goal by empowering the people to achieve the vision God has given you to plant a new church.

STARTING AND GROWING

Church planting involves both starting new churches and growing them. Starting a new church is like having a baby. When the new church plant is like an infant, it will require lots of nurture and care. The work of church planting doesn't stop once a church is planted, but carries on throughout the life of the new church. The evolution of the church involves growing disciples by developing systems and structures for spiritual growth. Therefore, the church-planting strategy must be organic and focus on both starting and growing a new church from beginning to end.

JESUS' PROMISE TO BUILD HIS CHURCH

Church planting reminds us that Jesus is the author and finisher of our faith and He is the One who builds His church. Jesus told Peter, "I tell you that you are Peter, and on this rock I will build my church, and the gates of Hades will not overcome it" (Matt. 16:18 NIV). Church planting begins and ends with Jesus Christ. The word "Christian" carries the meaning of being Christ-like. Therefore, a proper Christology is the place to start if we are really going to plant new churches.

I have seen a lot of church planters think that the church belongs to them, but nothing could damage the church more than this belief! Church leaders can use church-growth principles to plant churches, but only Christ can save and grow people into disciples of Jesus Christ. As you seek to plant a new church, don't ever forget that the new church belongs to Jesus Christ, and He is the One who will take care of it.

OBEDIENCE TO THE GREAT COMMISSION

As we discussed in the last chapter, one of the primary reasons for planting new churches is an act of obedience to "go therefore and make disciples of all the nations" (Matt. 28:19). When Jesus said, "make disciples," the disciples understood it to mean more than simply getting someone to believe in Jesus; they interpreted it to mean that they should make out of others what Jesus made out of them.

Don't ever forget that the goal of church planting is ultimately disciple making. Once you answer the call of God on your life, select a course of action, and then go for it! What do you have to lose? You will never know exactly what God can do until you step out in faith. The old Nike slogan says it all, "Just Do It"! God will lead and guide you as you begin to step out in faith. Beginning a new faith community is the key to reaching your city for Jesus Christ.

WAYS NEW CHURCHES ARE STARTED

Now that we have examined some definitions of church planting, it is important to ask the question: How are new churches started? While there are many different ways that new churches are started, I want to focus on several primary ways that church planting happens. The first way new churches are started is from what I call a denominational or network church plant. This is when a denomination or network identifies a planter and a location and offers assessment, training, and support to help start a new church.

One example of this is happening in the Church of England, where the Diocese of London has pledged to establish one hundred new worshipping communities in the diocese in the next five years. To help accomplish this vision, Ric Thorpe, who became bishop of Islington in September 2015, has developed a special focus on church planting in London.[7] Dozens of new churches are being started across England through these new initiatives. Some examples of new church plants in England are St. Thomas Norwich, which has grown from 50 to 450 in just two years and holds five services on Sundays, and KXC, in Kings Cross, London, which has grown to 500 worshipers since 2010.

Another example of how new churches are started is when a new church is birthed out of an existing church. This is called a "mother-daughter plant." In this model, the established church acts as a mother church offering financial, administrative, and relational support to the new church. The new church plant is a daughter congregation and usually stays in close relationship with the established church, especially in the first few years. The strength of this model is that the new plant has a sending church that offers support and connectivity to the planter and their team. One example of this is River Stone Church in Marietta, Georgia. Under the leadership of Tom Tanner, River Stone has helped give birth to six churches across the Northwest Metro Area. They plan to launch twenty like-minded, yet different-looking churches in this geographic area in the next ten years!

Another approach to church planting happens when church planters start a church by themselves. This is sometimes called the "parachute church plant," where the planter and their family move into a new community and start a new church. Sometimes the parachute planter doesn't have existing connections with a supporting church and moves into a new community with few if any connections and little support. The parachute church planter is often an apostolic leader like the apostle Paul who is comfortable starting something from nothing. This is clearly the hardest way to plant a new church; however, it can be done. Many church plants are started this way. In fact, the church we started in North Carolina was a parachute church plant that was very successful. However, while we started as an independent church, we quickly felt the need to be a part of a larger network of churches for support and encouragement.

Lead planters can either be bivocational or full-time workers in the church. There are strengths and weaknesses to both. Full-time time planters can focus the full amount of their energy on the new church. However, one of the challenges for a full-time church planter is building relationships with people who are not a part of the church. In fact, one of the greatest challenges new churches often face when starting out is how to reach unchurched people. Bivocational church planters work with people who are not in church and many times find it easier to build relationships with those who are not in the church. On the other hand, the greatest challenge for bi-vocational church planters is prioritizing and balancing schedules between family, work, and church, and poor time management can easily lead to burnout. Throughout the years I have spent in the world of church planting, I have seen and worked with both bivocational and full-time church planters who are very successful at what they do. Potential church planters should prayerfully consider which model is best for them.

A fourth way churches are planted is by teams. In many ways, healthy church plants are plants that start with teams, not individuals. Sadly, we often think of new churches as being led by a solo church planter who is like the lone ranger, but in reality, church planting is a team sport! Many times, church planters are portrayed as superhumans who can do everything without help, but nothing could be further from the truth. No one person can do all the work required to start a new church. It takes a team to plant a church, and it takes a church to make disciples.

In fact, new churches started by teams can have a higher success rate than those that don't. The reasons are numerous. Planting a church is hard work and can be a very lonely business because a church planter and his or her family often encounter difficulty in adjusting to a new cultural setting. In addition to this, planters may experience culture shock, spiritual warfare, spiritual fatigue, and even burnout. When planting a new church alone, there is also a lack of fellowship and accountability. Another one of the primary reasons why planting as teams is so successful is because a team approach allows multiple people to take responsibility for the success of the church, thus establishing a culture of discipleship and ownership rather than a culture of consumerism. Therefore, planning with a ministry team before you plant a church will go a long way in ensuring the long-term success of the church plant.

In conclusion, the foundation of church planting is the Great Commission and involves both evangelism and discipleship. We are called to plant new contextualized churches in every community, context, and part of the world. Malphurs's definition reminds us that the work of church planting is not easy, but it is an exciting venture of faith that is one of the primary ways to reach unchurched people with the gospel of Jesus Christ. However, we are all called to make and multiply disciples through planting new churches in every context. As we look at the next chapter, we will begin to explore some of the different models and ways that new churches are planted.

ESSENTIAL THOUGHT

Church planting is joining in God's mission to plant and multiply disciple-making churches in every context.

DISCUSSION QUESTIONS

1 Based on reading this chapter, what is a working definition of church planting?

2 Do you agree with the author's definition of church planting given in this chapter?

3 Would you define church planting differently?

4 How does church planting involve both evangelism and discipleship?

5 How has this chapter helped to clarify your understanding of what it means to plant a new church?

ACTION ITEMS

Do a prayer walk in your community. Ask the Holy Spirit to lead you to people, give you insight, and speak to you about a location.

Start a small group among people who are not currently in church. Invite them into your home for dinner. Listen to their stories, frustrations, fears, and dreams.

CHURCH PLANT PROFILE

Planter: **Jorge Acevedo**
Type: **Multi-site**
Church: **Grace Church**
Locations: **Cape Coral, Fort Myers Shores, Fort Myers Central, Fort Myers Trinity, and Sarasota, FL**

Jorge Acevedo was born in Puerto Rico and moved with his family to the United States at an early age. Jorge's life was touched by the grace of God at seventeen. Jorge, who was rescued from a life of addictions, believes his greatest delight is connecting people to Jesus and the church. Jorge tells the story:

> I had what you might call a nominal religious upbringing. Church was a very small part of my childhood, but I quit going to church when I was thirteen. The pastor yelled at me and my friend Alex for fooling around in the back of church during a service. I was so embarrassed that I left church that night and never returned to any church for five years. During those five years, my life spiraled into a world of drugs and alcohol. By the grace of God, a Campus Crusade for

Christ area director led me to Christ shortly before I graduated from high school.[1]

After answering the call to ministry, Jorge was appointed pastor of Grace Church in Cape Coral, Florida, in 1996. Under his able leadership, Grace Church has become a thriving, multi-site, United Methodist congregation in Southwest Florida with five campuses (Cape Coral, Fort Myers Shores, Fort Myers Central, Fort Myers Trinity, and Sarasota). Grace Church has grown in its weekend attendance from four hundred to more than twenty-six hundred in the past nineteen years.

Grace Church is recognized as having one of the largest and most effective recovery ministries in America, with more than seven hundred people involved in weekly meetings. In 2003, Grace Church planted a second campus in East Lee County by adopting a declining United Methodist church. Today this campus has more than 375 people in attendance. In 2007, Grace Church purchased a former grocery store and in November 2008, opened the Grace Community Center, a holistic ministry center and home to the third worshipping community of Grace Church. Jorge and Grace Church are an example of how God can multiply His church to reach a geographic region through multi-site church planting and multiplication. For more information about Jorge and Grace Church, visit http://www.egracechurch.com.

CHAPTER THREE

DISCOVERING MODELS

Church has to be planted, not cloned.
—Graham Cray

For many people, the topic of church planting can drum up images of a single way of starting a new church. However, I would expand the definition of church planting to include many different forms of birthing new faith communities. As I mentioned in the introduction, when it comes to church planting, one size doesn't fit all. There are many different types of new churches that are contextualized to a variety of different settings and cultures. Over the last ten years, I have had the privilege to work with many of these different types and models of church plants and each one is unique in its own fashion.

With regard to the diversity mentioned above, no one model is better than the other. Each one has the ability to be used by the Spirit as it adapts to fit a specific context. Neil Cole reminds us, "The answers are not found in our models, methods, and manmade systems but in the truth of God's Word and in being filled with the Spirit of God."[2] In order to best represent this diversity of models, I have written out a short list of several different types of church plants. Many of these models are focused on rapid multiplication and can be adapted to a variety of contexts. As you continue to explore church planting and your intended context, you will want to ask yourself: *What type of church will I plant?*

DIFFERENT MODELS OF CHURCH PLANTS

CONVENTIONAL CHURCH PLANT

The model that I title "traditional church planting" is a typical or established model of church planting that is focused on bringing together a large group of people for a worship gathering in a local community. I refer to this as a conventional church plant because it is one of the most common types of new churches. It often starts with a lead church planter who gathers a launch team of people prior to opening the church's worship service to the general public. While the traditional church plant meets in a larger worship gathering once a week (usually on Sunday morning), the church will also typically have small group meetings in peoples' homes throughout the week.

The launch team represents the foundation of the church and is composed of a core group of leaders. The launch members may join the team because of personal connections with the lead planter or they are sent from a sponsoring/mother church. The launch team members often serve on different ministry teams within the structure of the new community according to its mission plan. Typically, the conventional church plant model will require raising a significant amount of money for staffing, equipment, marketing, and facilities. The lead planter of a conventional church plant is often professionally trained and is usually either a full- to part-time paid staff member of the church. For more information about a conventional church-planting model, you can read Ed Stetzer and Daniel Im's *Planting Missional Churches* and Aubrey Malphurs's *The Nuts and Bolts of Church Planting.*

SIMPLE/HOUSE CHURCH

The simple/house church model is typically a small group (five to twenty people) that either meets in a home or another kind of intimate space such as a coffeehouse or even a local pub. These churches are called "simple" because they don't require the extensive staffing, buildings, or budgets that larger churches demand. Planting house churches is nothing new. From the very beginning of the Christian movement, we can see that the churches in the book of Acts were home churches. All across the globe, house churches naturally multiply rapidly as they focus on making disciples in intimate community. A wonderful example of a house church movement is Fuente De Avivamiento (Spring of Revival), which is led by my friend Dr. Iosmar Alvarez in Lexington, Kentucky. Prior to coming to the United States, Iosmar was a veterinary doctor turned church planter from Cuba. Since planting in Lexington, they have started nearly one hundred house churches that meet across the city!

While some house churches are autonomous, many are a part of a network of people meeting in homes throughout a city or geographic region. In some cases, the individual home churches are connected to a larger group of churches that meet together periodically in a collective setting. Personally, I know of several church planters who are planting simple house churches across their cities. This model requires very little funding and resourcing as there is no need to purchase or rent a meeting space, and the leaders of home churches are oftentimes bivocational. For more information about a simple/house church-planting model, you can read Neil Cole's *Organic Church* and J. D. Payne's *Missional House Churches*.

MISSIONAL COMMUNITIES

Another form of church planting that is beginning to take root in the United States and other countries is called missional communities. A missional community is typically a midsize group of people, about the size of an extended family (twenty to fifty people) who are united around a common mission and living out gospel community in "a particular neighborhood or network of relationships." Mike Breen has been an innovator in leading missional churches for more than twenty-five years. According to Breen, a missional community places a "strong value on life together, [and] the group has the expressed intention of seeing those they are in relationship with choose to start following Jesus through this more flexible and locally incarnated expression of the church."[3]

Many missional communities focus on living as a community together on mission in a decentralized, organic way to reach a city or community for Christ. Rather than inviting people to a service, they go to where the people are. Missional communities are rooted in a local parish neighborhood. In this sense, they are much more like a family of believers living out their faith incarnationally. One of the churches that I am helping with is a missional community. The church meets once a month for a corporate gathering, while the rest of the month the church meets in missional communities in local neighborhoods across the city of Lexington. For more information about missional communities you can read JR Woodward and Dan White Jr.'s book *The Church as Movement: Starting and Sustaining Missional-Incarnational Communities.*

SATELLITE/CAMPUS/MULTI-SITE

A model of church planting and multiplication that has really taken off in the last few years is the emergence of satellite/campus/multi-site congregations. This happens when an existing church opens new locations to expand into a different part of their city or geographic region. Some satellite/campus/multi-site congregations are even in another state! An example of a multi-site church is The Orchard in Tupelo, Mississippi. The Orchard was planted by Bryan Collier in 1998 and began with twenty-four people who met in a furniture warehouse with the goal of reaching people that no one else was reaching. "Our passion for church planting comes from our passion for lost people," Bryan said.[4] Seventeen years later, The Orchard has multiplied exponentially, with multiple sites in three communities, and averages 2,400 in weekly worship. They are already planning their ninth site!

Multi-site congregations are churches that progress from having one location to having multiple meeting sites so that they can reach more lost people. Some multi-site congregations are video venues that televise the teaching pastor from the main site to others, while other multi-site congregations have their own teaching pastors. Each location will typically have a site pastor who acts as the leader for that particular congregation. While they may be separate congregations, multi-site churches often share the same name, branding, financing, and even administrative support staffing to bring unity and continuity between each site. Multi-site congregations are one of the ways the Lord is using existing churches to reach beyond their local context! For more information about the multi-site church-planting model, you can read Geoff Surratt, Greg Ligon, and Warren Bird's *The Multi-Site Church Revolution.*

MULTICULTURAL/MULTIETHNIC CHURCH PLANTS

With more than 337 languages, the United States has become the most multicultural and multilingual nation on earth. The challenge of reaching the numerous people groups is a result of the growing diaspora from other nations who have come to North America. These men and women are often difficult to reach due to various language, cultural, and ethnic boundaries. As we witness the globalization of North America, the nations on continents such as Africa, Asia, and South America are beginning to send missionaries to re-evangelize the West through church planting! British author Martin Robinson talks about some of these church planters from developing countries who are now coming to the West.[5] They have come from nations like Brazil, Haiti, Mexico, Nigeria, Dominican Republic, and Ethiopia, just to name a few. As we view the very culture that surrounds us, we are instantly confronted with examples of a global issue.

As the West experiences globalization, a growing number of new churches are beginning to focus on reaching people from various nationalities and ethnic backgrounds. For instance, in many urban contexts, church plants will have to cross racial, cultural, and socioeconomic lines to reach their communities. One example is Anderson Moyo, who is pastor of a multi-ethnic church called Sheffield Community Church in England. Originally from Zimbabwe, Anderson has a heart not only for Europe, but also for the diaspora people of Africa who have come to England. He says, "We hope to train not only Africans, but emerging leaders from across the world as our denomination expands to new frontiers beyond the Western hemisphere."[6]

The apostle Paul reminds us, "I have become all things to all people, that by all means I might save some. I do it all for the sake of the gospel, that I may share with them in its blessings" (1 Cor. 9:22b–23 ESV). Multicultural/multiethnic church planting points to the beautiful picture promised in Revelation, where people from every nation, tribe, and language praise God in unison with one another. This portrait is essential to the Christian faith and no matter what kind of church we attend or are thinking about planting, we should all find ways to reach across ethnic, racial, cultural, and economic barriers. Multicultural/multiethnic church planting will be the future of church planting in North America and around the world. For more information about multiethnic church planting, you can read Mark DeYmaz's *Building a Healthy Multi-Ethnic Church.*

FRESH EXPRESSIONS

Fresh expressions are a new form of church planting in which I have become actively involved in recent years. The Fresh Expressions movement began in England more than a decade ago and has resulted in the birth of more than three thousand new communities alongside existing churches in the United Kingdom. It is beginning to take shape in other countries like the United States, Australia, Canada, and Germany. A fresh expression is "a form of church for our changing culture, established primarily for the benefit of people who are not yet members of any church."[7]

Every fresh expression is different because, "there is no single model to copy but a wide variety of approaches for a wide variety of contexts and constituencies. The emphasis is on planting something which is appropriate to its context, rather than cloning something which works elsewhere."[8] While each fresh expression of church is uniquely different, they come into being through principles of careful listening, service, contextual mission, and making disciples. God is using fresh expressions of church! According to the Church of England's research of the last two decades, they found the following:

40 percent of those who are a part of fresh expressions have no previous church background and for every person sent at least another two and a half are now present. That's a 250 percent increase over time![9]

There are endless examples of fresh expressions, such as dinner churches, biker churches, cowboy churches, even surfer churches like the one we started in Outer Banks, North Carolina. For more information about the Fresh Expressions model of church you can read Travis Collins's *Fresh Expressions of Church* and *From the Steeple to the Streets* or visit http://freshexpressionsus.org.

REPLANTING

Church planting entails creating a new congregation where none existed before, but a close relative of church planting is replanting or re-missioning existing churches. Replanting happens when a church that is in decline or dying decides to face their state and dares to start over again for the sake of advancing the gospel. Graham Singh, the executive director of Church Planting Canada, calls this a movement of "dead alive churches."[10]

Replanting requires churches to surrender and create a new identity, empower new leaders, and reach new people for Jesus. Rather than selling their buildings, in many cases older churches are opening their doors to allow new churches to be planted within their buildings and, thus, becoming a midwife for new churches. Replanting may also mean that a church sells their building and puts that money back into church planting. The reality is that very few churches have the honesty and humility to admit that their effectiveness is over and even fewer have the courage to do what it takes to replant. As you seek to participate in God's mission, pray and ask God if He may be leading you to guide existing churches in the direction of replanting. For more information about replanting, you can read Mark DeVine and Darrin Patrick's *Replant: How a Dying Church Can Grow Again.*

STRENGTHS AND WEAKNESSES OF MODELS

Regardless of the approach or model, church planting is one of the greatest ways to make disciples. In the end, starting new churches will require Christians to think outside of the box and to engage their culture with the gospel of Christ in fresh new ways. Theologian Francis Schaeffer reminds us, "Every generation of Christians has this problem of learning how to speak meaningfully to its own age. It cannot be solved without an understanding of the changing existential situation which it faces."[11] We should all share in the responsibility of impacting the nations for Christ through planting new churches, establishing fresh expressions, or replanting existing churches.

As we close this chapter, it is important to note that there are strengths and weaknesses of church-planting models. A model is simply a tool to accomplish the goal of starting a new church. Don't confuse a model with a cookie-cutter, one-size-fits-all way of planting a new church for every context. Every context is different—what works in Africa may not work in Ireland, etc. What works in one place may not work in another. Every context, every church planter, and every new church is different. Therefore, you must take into consideration the context and culture of the community where you are seeking to plant the church, as well as the unique gifts and calling of the church planter and their teams to decide what model works best for you. No one model of church planting is right or wrong, because each church plant is unique. Many times new churches are a hybrid of various models and influences. The important thing is that you ask the Lord to guide and direct you in what type of church He is calling you to plant to reach unchurched people in your community.

ESSENTIAL THOUGHT

When it comes to church planting,
there are a variety of models and
methods that need to fit the context.

DISCUSSION QUESTIONS

1   When it comes to church planting, one size doesn't fit all. What are your thoughts about the variety of church-planting models?

2   Which model of church planting best fits your context?

3   Are you envisioning a different kind of church-planting model than one which was discussed in the chapter?

4   What are the benefits of examining church-planting models?

5   What are the potential downsides of looking at church-planting models?

ACTION ITEMS

Visit three different church plants in your geographic area and then compare and contrast the differences between them. Identify strengths and weaknesses. What can you learn from them?

Take a church planter to lunch or coffee to ask them questions and learn from their successes and failures.

CHURCH
PLANT
PROFILE

Planter:	**Luke Edwards**
Type:	**Fresh Expression**
Church:	**King Street Church**
Location:	**Boone, NC**

Luke Edwards planted King Street Church as a new fresh expression of church out of Boone United Methodist Church in 2013. Boone UMC wanted to reach those on the margins of their community and so they commissioned the birth of King Street Church. "We felt like the church was called to do more than serve," Luke Edwards, pastor of King Street Church, said. "We're called to welcome, include, and worship with everyone. We still excluded the marginalized from the body because we served them, but didn't welcome them."[1]

When examining what model or approach they were going to take for the new church, they chose to follow the Fresh Expressions model. Fresh Expressions focuses on one aspect of the church, such as prayer or worship, and adds additional pieces until the group forms a mature expression of the body of Christ. They've found that these new ways of presenting the traditional gospel make it easier for those unfamiliar with church to become a faith community.

In the beginning, Luke approached a few people exploring the Christian faith, but who were not necessarily Christians. This group of five to six spent three months eating together during the course of one summer. Gradually, this group became a community that worshipped together and dialogued about faith and life. King Street Church was born. Now, that group meets weekly in what they call Sundays at the Saloon. On Sunday evenings, Christians and non-Christians alike gather to read a passage of Scripture, apply it to their lives, ingest it, and wash it down with a cold beer.

Daniel, a former inmate in the Watauga County Jail, is one of many who reconnected with Jesus through this fresh expression of church. Although Daniel grew up in the church, he became disconnected during his incarceration. After his release, he felt intimidated to return because of his past. Yet, God still had a plan for Daniel. About a year and a half ago, Daniel started coming to King Street Church's service in the Boone Saloon. He quickly became one of the central leaders and is using his experiences to broaden the church's ministry to include those still incarcerated or recently released.

King Street now offers a variety of gatherings designed with a specific group of people in mind. These include a ministry to inmates in the Watauga County Jail, college students, the homeless, businesspersons, service projects, the Single Mom Squad, and Death Café, which encourages open, honest conversations about death. For more information on Luke and King Street Church, visit **http://asburyseminary .edu/voices/luke-edwards**.

CHAPTER FOUR

THE DNA OF A NEW CHURCH

Mission is the DNA of the church.
—William O'Brien

If you were to walk to your car right now and open up the hood, you would be confronted with a mass of metal, wiring, plastic, tubes, and valves. For the average person, this jumbled mess represents the driving force of the car: the engine. But to the trained eye, this overwhelming conglomeration of stuff represents intricate relationships that form the whole of the engine. Each part plays a role, and if one part is missing, the engine no longer functions at full capacity or at all! In fact, many of these elements in engines are universal to all brands of engines and they are crucial to an engine's function. In the same way, the whole of a church is formed by numerous pieces that function as one body. While each church may be unique in its own right, all churches share certain pillars that constitute a thriving body.

As I have said throughout the book, it will take all kinds of churches to reach all kinds of people: large churches, small churches, traditional churches, nontraditional churches,

DNA of a New Church

churches being planted on college campuses, prisons, storefronts, coffeehouses, and homes. Although contexts may change, I do believe that there are common biblical patterns or DNA that new churches hold in common. In this chapter, we will explore the essential, replicable elements that are common to healthy new churches. I have primarily drawn these seven essentials from the book of Acts—which is our very first church-planting manual—and from my personal experience and research in studying church-planting movements, especially the Wesleyan revival of the eighteenth and nineteenth centuries.[2]

The Wesleyan revival, which started with only a handful of people in the 1700s, grew into a movement that established hundreds of societies in England and the United States. By the time of John Wesley's death in 1791, Methodism had become a global church movement with more than seventy thousand members in England and more than forty thousand in the new United States and other mission stations around the world. The growth of Methodism continued well beyond the life of John Wesley. Under the leadership of Francis Asbury, Methodism in North America grew from 1,200 to 200,000 members strong, with more than four thousand preachers.[3] Then, from 1850 to 1905, American Methodism averaged planting more than seven hundred churches per year.[4] In particular, I believe that the wisdom of the Wesleyan revival offers seven simple essentials that you will need as you begin planting a new church.

CHRIST-CENTERED

Christ is the foundation and the reason why we plant churches. The foundation of church planting and the entire Christian faith is Jesus Christ, and removing Him as this foundation is the most crippling error any church can commit. Sadly, I have seen people try to plant churches for many different reasons. Some have tried to plant out of pride, some for fame or recognition, and others have tried to plant churches out of strife or envy. These methods lead to disaster because Christ must be the reason for and the foundation of every new church plant. As we review Scripture, we see that Christ is the cornerstone (see Ephesians 2:20) and the establisher (see Matthew 16:18) of the church. Make sure that your church-planting endeavors are built upon the solid rock of Christ.

On a more personal level, when we look at the pages of church history, we see that every major Christian movement begins with a life-changing encounter with the living Christ. In his book *Movements That Change the World*, Steve Addison asserted, "History is made by men and women of faith who have met with the living God."[5] Think about it. Moses met with God in the burning bush. Paul encountered Christ on the road to Damascus. Wesley encountered Christ at Aldersgate. Augustine encountered God under a tree. Luther encountered Christ in the Bible. Saint Francis encountered God at the cross. Saint Patrick encountered God in a dream.

Church history is full of stories of individuals who had a life-transforming experience with the risen Christ that left them forever changed. Are we any better or different than these pillars of history? I think not! We must have the same life-changing encounter with Christ that inspired the great heroes of the faith if we are going to plant churches.

Christ, however, isn't just the organizational foundation of the church and its members; He is also the message that is proclaimed. Upon departing for America, Thomas Coke asked John Wesley what message he should proclaim. Wesley responded by saying, "Offer them Christ." As church planters, we have nothing to offer people but Jesus Christ. Our call is to offer them Christ. In the burning words of John Wesley, "You have nothing to do but to save souls. Therefore spend and be spent in this work. And go not only to those that need you, but to those that need you most."[6] When starting a new church, make sure that Christ is the center of everything that you do and everything that you teach.

SPIRIT-EMPOWERED

The early church came alive and grew exponentially after the Holy Spirit came upon them on the Day of Pentecost (see Acts 1:8). It is impossible to understand the explosive growth of the Wesleyan revival without understanding the important role of the Holy Spirit in the lives of individuals, lay ministers, and the establishing of new churches. In many ways, the Methodist movement was a unique work of the Holy Spirit. Along with others, John and Charles Wesley helped establish the Fetter Lane Society in May 1738 for the purpose of discipleship and accountability. The Holy Spirit showed up one night at the Fetter Lane Society in a powerful way. John Wesley recorded the encounter in his journal on January 1, 1739:

> Mr. Hall, Hinching, Ingham, Whitefield, Hutching, and my brother Charles were present at our love feast in Fetter Lane with about 60 of our brethren. About three in the morning, as we were continuing instant in prayer, the power of God came mightily upon us insomuch that many cried out for exceeding joy and many fell to the ground. As soon as we were recovered a little from that awe and amazement at the presence of His majesty, we broke out with one voice, "We praise Thee, O God, we acknowledge Thee to be the Lord."[7]

Church planting is hard work and you cannot and should not attempt to do it in your own strength or understanding. If we are going to plant churches in the twenty-first century, we need a fresh touch of the power and presence of the Holy Spirit. Without the Holy Spirit, there can be no church because the church is the community of the Spirit. Therefore, without the Holy Spirit, there cannot begin any genuine church-planting endeavors.

As a church planter, it is vital that you have a personal, ongoing experience of the Holy Spirit. Don't be ashamed to ask for the Holy Spirit to give you power to be a witness, because it's a biblical promise. In Acts, the church prayed, "grant to Your servants that with all boldness they may speak Your word" and then it says that when they finished praying "they were all filled with the Holy Spirit, and they spoke the word of God with boldness" (Acts 4:29, 31). Ask the Lord for boldness, open your heart, and let the Holy Spirit give you power to do His work. This means that we are to surrender our lives daily and yield ourselves to the Spirit's influence and guidance. Church planting is tough sometimes, and the indwelling of the Spirit is the only power through which God has called us to do work.

LAY LEADERSHIP

The explosive growth of the early church can be explained in only one way: lay leadership. On the Day of Pentecost three thousand were added to the church and they began to meet in home gatherings that were led by lay people. The role of lay people in the life and mission of a new church cannot be over-estimated. Regardless of the context, there is nothing more powerful than when ordinary men and women do the effective work of ministry in a new church.

Significant movements such as the Wesleyan revival were built on lay leadership. As Methodism grew, Wesley saw the need to appoint lay preachers to assist him in preaching the gospel to the masses. This was a bold decision on Wesley's part because it meant breaking from the traditional view that only the ordained clergy could preach the gospel and do ministry. Part of Wesley's genius was his ability to select, train, and gather lay leaders around him who became extensions of his own personal vision. The rapid and miraculous growth of Methodism would not have been possible without the endeavors and self-sacrifice of those early Methodist lay leaders. John Wesley famously said in a letter, "Give me one hundred preachers who fear nothing but sin and desire nothing but God, and I care not a straw whether they be clergymen or laymen, such alone will shake the gates of hell and set up the kingdom of heaven upon earth."[8] The truth of the 1700s remains the same today: we need both ordained and lay people to plant new churches in the twenty-first century.

Today one of the most common features of church-planting movements around the world is lay leadership, not professional clergy. David Garrison, who is a pioneer in the understanding of church-planting movements, said, "In church planting movements the laity are clearly in the driver's seat. Unpaid, non-professional common men and women are leading the churches. . . . Lay leadership is firmly grounded in the doctrine of the priesthood of the believer—the most egalitarian doctrine ever set forth."[9] Therefore, when planning on starting a new church, build it on a model that empowers and releases lay leadership for ministry and evangelism.

INTENTIONAL DISCIPLESHIP

For a new church to be healthy and grow, it must develop an intentional and natural process for making disciples that involves small groups. Disciples are made through building a biblical, Christ-centered community. When reading the book of Acts, we can see that the life of the early church revolved around community that happened in small group gatherings in homes. Community is an intimate union in which Christians can share. This is not just friendship, but a deep bond that only Christians can know as the family of God. The Christian life consists of living together in community with one another and Christ.

John Wesley can also teach us about the importance of small-group discipleship. He organized the people into class meetings to encourage and nurture believers in the faith. He knew that preaching was not enough to keep people in the faith. Wesley gathered people in small groups called "class meetings" to meet weekly for prayer, instruction, and mutual fellowship. Each group was about twelve in number with one leader who was either a man or a woman. The leaders served their group with a kind of pastoral oversight. These groups met the various needs of the people who attended them. He described these societies in the following way, "Such a society is no other than a company of men having the form and seeking the power of godliness, united in order to pray together, to receive the word of exhortation, and to watch over one another in love, that they may help each other to work out their salvation."[10]

Practically speaking, small groups are one of the most effective ways that churches have used to make disciples. The Christian life finds its fulfillment when we share it together with one another and in Christ. Small groups provide a place for spiritual growth, intimacy, accountability, and protection. The church is not a building but the family of God and the body of Christ. The people that we connect with in small groups become our spiritual family that support and encourage us. Through true fellowship in small groups, we experience and share the love of God with our brothers and sisters in Christ. These groups become atmospheres where spiritual formation is actualized through fellowship.

SPIRITUAL PRACTICES

We all have rhythms, routines, and rituals that make up our daily lives. We are creatures of habit. Many of us wake up in the morning, drink a cup of coffee, brush our teeth, and read our newspaper. Or maybe we start the day off with a simple prayer and Bible reading. Routines and rituals are not a bad thing. They keep us on track and remind us of what matters most. Spiritual practices are rhythms of grace that help us grow in our daily walk with Christ. Encouraging your church members to embrace and practice the means of grace will help them integrate their faith into their daily lives.

The church in Acts was committed to regular spiritual practices: "to the apostles' teaching and to fellowship, to the breaking of bread and to prayer" (Acts 2:42 NIV). John Wesley called these spiritual practices the means of grace. He said, "The chief of these means are prayer, whether in secret or with the great congregation; searching the Scriptures; (which implies reading, hearing, and meditating thereon); and receiving the Lord's supper, eating bread and drinking wine in remembrance of him: And these we believe to be ordained of God, as the ordinary channels of conveying his grace to the souls of men."[11] The means of grace are spiritual practices and ways that God provides spiritual growth for believers. Many of these God-given means have been lost to the church of today and desperately need to be recovered.

The means of grace are essential to the life and health of all believers and should be taught from the very beginning at a new church. These means include personal and corporate spiritual practices that promote spiritual growth in keeping with Paul's command to "discipline yourself for the purpose of godliness" (1 Tim. 4:7 NASB). The word "discipline" literally means "exercise," and spiritual disciplines are essentially spiritual exercises. Just as physical exercise promotes strength in the body, the spiritual practices promote godliness and growth in grace. They are vital to the individual and to the community as it seeks to become more like Christ.

Disciples must live a life that is committed to the ongoing practice of spiritual disciplines. Discipleship doesn't just happen. This means that the Christian faith is more than a theory that is taught in a classroom, but something that is practiced in everyday life. Discipleship should always be practical and applied to real life. Spiritual disciplines are not for a select group of people or scholars, but for all Christians, whether they be pastors, professors, or plumbers. Let's commit ourselves to the process of discipleship by practicing spiritual disciplines in our everyday life.

HOLISTIC MISSION

Central to the life of the new church in the book of Acts is a holistic mission. Theologian Emil Brunner reminds us, "The Church exists by mission, just as fire exists by burning."[12] Holistic mission means that we look outwardly by being both evangelistic and socially minded. It means that we care about people's souls and their bodies. It means that because we care about the gospel, we should care about social and environmental issues. Holistic mission brings all of life together under the banner of the gospel of Jesus Christ.

Holistic mission is God's way of showing the love of His Son Jesus through His church. Christians must strive to always be like Jesus, our perfect example. Jesus said, "the Son of Man did not come to be served, but to serve, and to give His life a ransom for many" (Mark 10:45). This Scripture beautifully embodies the task of Christian ministry. To be a Christian is to be a servant. We are to serve and give our lives for others. Serving is the example that Jesus gave. We should follow it. The church I planted in the Outer Banks of North Carolina taught me the powerful meaning of holistic mission. The church was involved in several community outreaches to build bridges to reach the unchurched people in our community in a number of creative ways. We adopted beach accesses, which the church cleaned once a month to show the community that the church cares about the beaches. The church began an art-mentoring program that has reached hundreds of at-risk youth in our community and in South America. The church also hosts quarterly art shows that infuse art, music, and coffee. These community art shows draw hundreds of people from the community. We eventually opened an art gallery that hosts art shows and concerts to build bridges between the church and community.

Holistic mission also involves recovering biblical hospitality. Many contemporary Christians and churches have lost touch with biblical hospitality. It is imperative that we relearn the gift of hospitality, especially in light of its important place in the Scriptures. The word "hospitality" literally means "love of strangers" and is found several times in the New Testament (see Romans 12:13; 1 Timothy 3:2; Titus 1:8; 1 Peter 4:9). Saint Benedict reminds us in his Rule, "Let all guests who arrive be received like Christ, for he is going to say, 'I came as a guest, and you received me.'"[13] We are all called to offer the love of Christ to our guests and welcome them in such a way that they would be transformed from strangers into friends. A new church is a wonderful place to recover the lost art of hospitality and sharing God's gifts with the world.

REPRODUCING CULTURE

Wherever the gospel is firmly planted, the seed will grow and multiply. The book of Acts demonstrates that authentic Christianity cannot be contained but reproduces rapidly like a virus from one person to another. As we saw in the beginning of the chapter, the Methodist movement spread rapidly throughout the British Isles and North America. Methodism was a multiplication movement that reproduced everything: disciples, leaders, small groups, and societies.

To keep up with the growth, they planted hundreds of new societies around the world. Societies were essentially like new churches that were planted in geographic centers and would quickly reproduce by planting other societies in neighboring areas and towns to reach even more people with the gospel. Wesley carefully chose, appointed, and empowered those who would lead these societies. They were men and women of piety and experience, and Wesley's careful selection solidified the growth of the movement. As a result, Wesleyan societies began to multiply and continued to grow rapidly throughout England. Everywhere they went, societies were created to keep and nurture new converts. As a result of this intentional discipleship, the number of Methodists grew at an amazing rate from a handful of people to thousands (if not millions!) of followers.

There is much we can learn about contemporary church planting by looking to past movements such as the Wesleyan revival. As we've just explored, although every church is different, healthy new churches share a common DNA. From Christ-centeredness to a missional focus, new plants are reaching outside the traditional walls of the church to build bridges with people who are not a part of the institutional church. As you begin to think through the process of planting a new church, envision how you can cultivate and encourage each of the common essentials mentioned in this chapter.

ESSENTIAL THOUGHT

Although contexts may change, there are universal biblical patterns that successful new churches share.

DISCUSSION QUESTIONS

1 What are some of the common essentials of a new church?

2 Do you agree with the author's premise that while context may change, there are common biblical patterns that new churches share?

3 Are there some common patterns that are missing from this chapter? If so, take a few minutes to discuss them.

4 How and why should Christ be the center of every part of a new church's life?

5 How is discipleship an essential of church planting, no matter what the context?

ACTION ITEMS

Develop an ongoing relationship with church planters in your area. Join a learning community of church planters or missional Christians.

Take a few hours and begin to work through the strategic plan in the back of the book. If you have a team, work through the plan together.

CHURCH PLANT PROFILE

Planter:	**Carolyn Moore**
Type:	**Traditional/Female Church Planter**
Church:	**Mosaic United Methodist**
Location:	**Evans, GA**

Carolyn Moore is an author, speaker, and founding pastor of Mosaic United Methodist Church. In June of 2003, she was appointed to the Augusta area, where she and her family helped give birth to Mosaic United Methodist Church, a church that focuses on reaching people in the margins. In more than ten years of weekly worship, Mosaic has seen more than 130 baptisms and hundreds of professions of faith.

Carolyn describes the vision of the church in the following way,

> *Our vision at Mosaic is to make room for those in the margins as we serve together in mission. We have baptized nearly two hundred adults since the inception of our church and have seen hundreds come to faith in Christ. We have a strong commitment to healing and discipleship and are raising up new leaders for the body of Christ. Having experienced the challenges of entrepreneurial ministry, I learned early*

on that my calling and authority must be rooted in an ongoing personal encounter with Christ. That pursuit of personal holiness is central to our life and ministry together. As we say often in our church, if Jesus isn't in it, we're not interested.[1]

After more than ten years, Mosaic is a continuing example of a new church that is reaching broken lives with the love of Jesus. Carolyn's unique calling and gifts are a wonderful example for other women who feel called to planting. Carolyn reflects on her journey and wants to share it with others,

Now that I have had the remarkably rewarding experience of seeing a church grow from three souls (the sum of my immediate family members) to a place of health and vitality, I have a great desire to see other women enter the journey of church planting with better mentors, training, resources and support. I want the voices they hear to be voices of encouragement and confidence so the Kingdom can come to earth as it is in heaven.[2]

For more information about Carolyn and Mosaic, visit **http://asburyseminary.edu/voices/carolyn-moore.**

CHAPTER FIVE

MAKING AND MULTIPLYING DISCIPLES

The church has tried to get world evangelization without disciple making.
—Bill Hull

The church in much of the Western world is experiencing a discipleship crisis, and we are seeing the fallout from this deficiency. At the First International Consultation on Discipleship, John Stott called attention to the "strange and disturbing paradox" of the contemporary Christian situation. He warned, "We have experienced enormous statistical growth without corresponding growth in discipleship. God is not pleased with superficial discipleship."[3] Sadly, some churches focus on evangelism at the expense of discipleship by seeking to win converts instead of making disciples, despite the fact that the goal of evangelism is disciple making.[4]

The reality is the Great Commission involves both evangelism and discipleship. Dallas Willard called this unity "discipleship evangelism."[5] Evangelism and discipleship are two sides of the same coin and cannot be separated. Evangelism is the beginning of the journey and discipleship is the process of spiritual growth. The church needs to rediscover the integrative process that focuses on serious disciple making, not just leading people to make a decision in order to fulfill the Great Commission.[6] The Great Commission compels Christians to focus on keeping people through discipleship as much as they focus on reaching people through evangelism.

It is important to differentiate between being a person who is a Christian in name only and a disciple of Jesus Christ. Alan Hirsch said, "We can't make disciples based on a consumerist approach to the faith. We plainly cannot consume our way into discipleship . . . Consumption is detrimental to discipleship."[7] The result of consumerism on Christianity is what Dietrich Bonhoeffer called "cheap grace" in his most famous work, *The Cost of Discipleship*, first published in 1939.

Many professing Christians in North America are not disciples according to the New Testament definition. One survey concludes that only 25 percent of evangelicals meet the biblical standard for a disciple.[8] In *Growing True Disciples*, researcher George Barna reported that the church in America is comprised of "many converts, but shockingly few disciples."[9]

In a similar way, Dallas Willard illustrated the lack of discipleship in the United States in the following way:

The leading assumption in the American church is that you can be a Christian but not a disciple. That has placed a tremendous burden on a mass of Christians who are not disciples. We tell them to come to church, participate in our programs, and give money. But we see a church that knows nothing of commitment. We have settled for the marginal, and so we carry this awful burden of trying to motivate people to do what they don't want to do. We can't think about church the way we have been. We need to clear our heads about what discipleship is. My definition: A disciple is a person who has decided that the most important thing in their life is to learn how to do what Jesus said to do.[10]

DISCIPLE-MAKING REVOLUTION

Church planting is ultimately a revolutionary call for the universal church to return to a serious and intentional discipleship! Making disciples is the call of every Christian and ultimately the call of every new church. The word "disciple" comes from the Greek word *mathetes*, which is found 269 times in the New Testament and means an "apprentice, learner, or a pupil." In the ancient times of the Bible, a disciple was a person who left everything that they had to follow the teachings of a master. The word "disciple" implies much more than a learner or a pupil; it is someone who has totally committed his or her life to the training and teaching of a master or a school of thought. According to the New Testament, a disciple is a born-again believer who is obedient, bears fruit, glorifies God, has joy, loves others, denies themselves, and is committed to fulfilling the Great Commission (see John 3:3–8; 15:7–17; Luke 9:23–25; Matthew 28:19).

So what is discipleship? Discipleship is simply answering the call of Christ to, "Go and make disciples." Discipleship is an organic process of helping others become and continue to be disciples of Jesus Christ. Discipleship is not a program that has a beginning and an ending point. We should spend as much, if not more, of our time, resources, and energy focusing on discipleship as much as we do on evangelism. Christians need to reevaluate the New Testament model of discipleship for twenty-first-century ministry. Likewise, individual churches should seek to develop organic discipleship models that are biblically faithful and culturally relevant to their particular context of ministry.

The beauty about church planting is that it is all about making and multiplying disciples. This is the result of selecting, training, and empowering leaders who will, in turn, reproduce themselves in others. This begins locally with the church and then can take place on a larger scale through reproduction of church plants regionally and internationally. Just think, through a faithful commitment to investing in others, you can be a part of a twenty-first-century, disciple-making movement that can change our postmodern world for Christ!

But how do we accomplish this goal of reproductive discipleship? Naturally, the most powerful paradigm for forming disciples is the discipleship methodology of Jesus. In *The Master Plan of Evangelism*, Robert Coleman told us that Jesus' plan of reproducing disciples "was not with programs to reach the multitudes but with men whom the multitudes would follow . . . [people] were to be His method of winning the world to God. The initial objective of Jesus' plan was to enlist men who could bear witness to His life and carry on His work after He returned to the Father."[11] If we are to be like Jesus, we must invest our lives in faithful followers who will in turn invest themselves in others.

The Master Plan of Evangelism has been used by millions of Christians around the world to make disciples. The book is especially helpful for new churches that are seeking to fulfill the Great Commission. In fact, it was the foundational text that we used when we planted our church in North Carolina. Coleman's watershed book offers the following eightfold way Jesus trained the twelve disciples: selection, association, consecration, impartation, demonstration, delegation, supervision, and reproduction. In this section, I will summarize Coleman's analysis of Jesus' training of the twelve disciples and apply it to reproducing disciples and building teams in a new church plant.

SELECTION

It all started when Jesus called a few men to follow Him. Jesus did not choose everyone He met to be His disciples. He took very seriously the selection of men He trained. Rather than focusing on the multitude, He only chose twelve. The reason for His selectivity was intentional. He chose twelve men to instruct and train, who would, in time, reproduce themselves in others. A few good men were Jesus' master plan of reproducing disciples.

In a similar way, we too must be selective in whom we choose to disciple. We should look for people who are faithful, willing, and able to continue the chain of discipleship. Discipleship does not require a degree or Bible college education, but simply obedience and investment. We should seek to find men and women who have a passion and a hunger for Christ, because willingness to answer the call to follow Jesus is the only requirement to be a disciple of Jesus.

ASSOCIATION

Jesus was intimately involved in the lives of His disciples as they followed Him. His training method was spending time with His disciples in order to build deep relationships with them. Coleman pointed out that Jesus had no formal training or education. He was His own school and curriculum. This is a radical concept for those of us who live in the twenty-first century. Whenever we find someone who seems called into ministry, we send them off to let someone else train them. However, the New Testament model of discipleship was home-grown, natural, and organic. In reality, discipleship happens as men and women spend time with their spiritual mentor.

In a similar way, we should be present in the lives of the people we are seeking to develop. We should schedule time with people whom we want to disciple outside of normal church functions. This time can include times of play, prayer, and sharing meals together. This means that discipleship will require something of us. As with any worthwhile investment, discipleship costs us something. We must sacrifice our time, energy, and emotion for the sake of others if we are to fulfill the demanding task of making disciples. I believe this is one of the number-one reasons that churches don't disciple anymore: for many, discipleship demands too high of a price. But this is a price we must pay if we are going to build healthy and thriving churches that serve the Lord faithfully.

CONSECRATION

When Jesus called His followers, He expected them to obey Him. He sought to create in His disciples a lifestyle of consecrated obedience. Discipleship is about a total consecration to the Lord. As disciples, we need to submit and obey God's Word and plan for our lives. However, many of us have trouble submitting, and we instead return to a lifestyle that models an individualistic culture where people do not want to submit to authority. That is why submission and obedience to God is so hard as well as important. When we become obedient to God in every area of our lives, we will experience victorious Christian living. God can only use men and women who are willing to obey Him above all else.

IMPARTATION

Jesus gave Himself away to His disciples by imparting to them everything that the Father had given to Him. He gave Himself freely by not only imparting Himself, but also spiritual truth about life and ministry. He taught them about the Scriptures and the Holy Spirit through both His words and His actions. Just as Jesus imparted Himself to His disciples, we must seek to give ourselves to the men and women that we are called to serve. We must be conduits through which God can transfer His wisdom and character as true discipleship takes place. As leaders, it is important for us to grasp that we have a spiritual responsibility to impart ourselves to others if we are going to make disciples.

DEMONSTRATION

One reason Jesus had such a lasting impact on His disciples is that He lived the message before them daily. He was the message and the method. By walking with Jesus, they saw how He lived His faith in the real world. He prayed before them. He fed the poor. He had compassion on the multitude. He healed the sick. In other words, He lived the life that He wanted to reproduce in His disciples. After Jesus' death and resurrection, He expected His disciples to say and do what He said and did, and the book of Acts tells us that they did just as He modeled.

It is important that we practice what we preach, because the people we are training will follow our life and example. It is not enough to preach the gospel; we have to practice it daily. Our personal walk with God is one of the most important factors in developing godly leaders. We will reproduce what we are. The most powerful message is a life lived for God. Make sure that the life you live is worthy for others to follow.

DELEGATION

Jesus assigned His disciples work. He developed His disciples by delegating ministry responsibilities to them. He sent His disciples out and gave them ministry responsibilities where failure was a real possibility. Hands-on experience was a vital part of Jesus' discipleship curriculum. It is funny that churches make people do things that even Jesus did not do. Some churches make people go through a yearlong process before they can even serve in any capacity in the church. Likewise, some people spend years in college and seminary with little if any real ministry involvement. Churches need to rethink delegating spiritual responsibility to people, especially new believers. Is it any wonder our discipleship is often anemic? Sadly, most people think the pastor is supposed to do everything in the church. We must not forget the power of involving people in ministry.

SUPERVISION

Supervision is important in helping others improve and grow in their service. Jesus supervised His disciples and whenever they returned from a ministry trip, they would report to Him what they had done. This allowed a time for the disciples to reflect, review, and to receive instruction from Jesus. Supervision is an important part of leadership development, especially when dealing with new believers. We want to delegate and empower people to act, but we also need to help supervise them to make sure they stay on track. Many times, people will get into trouble without proper supervision. Supervision is ultimately an art. On the one hand, if we are not careful, we can micromanage people. On the other hand, we can be so loose that we don't supervise people at all.

REPRODUCTION

Jesus expected His disciples to reproduce His likeness in others. He imparted His message and mission to His disciples so that they would reproduce themselves in others and make disciples of all nations. The Great Commission implies that the followers of Jesus will reproduce themselves and "make disciples."

Reproduction is how the Christian movement was born. Today, what has become a 2.1 billion-member movement started with only twelve disciples. Consider the analogy of the Vine in John 15:1–17. The purpose of the Vine (Jesus) and the branches (us) is to bear fruit. Christians are to work for and expect a harvest (see Matthew 9:37–38; Luke 10:2). Let us commit our lives and our churches to reproducing ourselves in others in order to make and multiply disciples of our communities and our world.

BECOMING A DISCIPLE-MAKING CHURCH

I want to end this chapter by offering some practical examples and ways for how new churches can develop discipleship processes that can be tailored to fit unique contexts. New churches need to think critically about creating a discipleship process that leads people from conversion to becoming fully devoted followers of Jesus Christ from the very beginning. There is no greater model for discipleship than that of Jesus Christ Himself and, as seen above, *The Master Plan of Evangelism* offers great insight that we can tap into. If you haven't already, I would highly recommend that you take your church leadership team through *The Master Plan of Evangelism* and develop a unique discipleship process for your new church that seeks to connect new believers to the church and grow them into disciples who will reproduce themselves by making future disciples. If you do not start your church doing the hard work of creating disciples from the very beginning, your church will be in jeopardy of being ineffective. Or worse yet, you will end up making consumers, not disciples. Let us fight against this norm of Western Christianity and answer the call of Jesus Christ to "go and make disciples" in and through our new churches.

ONE-ON-ONE DISCIPLESHIP

There are several primary ways in which your new church can make disciples. First, train leaders in the art of one-on-one intentional discipleship. As we have seen from *The Master Plan of Evangelism*, Jesus focused most heavily on the few and not the multitude. The beauty of this approach is that one-on-one discipleship is simple and doesn't require a curriculum or seminary degree, it just takes time and a commitment to building relationships. This can take place by meeting in ordinary places like coffee shops and office break rooms. As leaders of the new church, one-on-one discipleship allows you to model disciple making as Jesus did for his disciples.

One-on-one discipleship takes time to build trust and relationships and can't be rushed, but it takes into account a trend that few contemporary Christians grasp: discipleship begins not with conversion, but oftentimes precedes it. Think for a moment about when you became a Christian. What events, people, or circumstances led you to that point? Who shared their faith with you? How long did the process take? In chapter 1 I introduced you to Adam, who came to faith in our church. The real story wasn't when he came to faith, but the countless hours of one-on-one discipleship that began before and continued after he came to faith. The reality is, very little of his discipleship took place in a church building. We spent time together in the coffeeshop, at the beach surfing together, and at dinner with our families. Through perseverance and commitment, one-on-one discipleship lays a firm foundation for those seeking to devote their lives to Christ.

SMALL GROUP DISCIPLESHIP

Second, every new church should begin by starting and multiplying small groups. Small groups are an important way to help people build authentic gospel-centered disciples by offering accountability and community. Small groups provide ways to connect and grow disciples with the gospel through Bible studies, pathways to serve, and teaching spiritual disciplines. Small groups consist of ten to fifteen people who come together regularly for prayer, Scripture reading, accountability, and fellowship. As with the various types of church plants, there are all kinds of groups because there are all kinds of people. There can be small groups for married couples, single adults, blended groups, men's groups, and women's groups just to name a few. Groups can be designed for new Christians or for those who want to really dig deeper into a book of the Bible. There can be a small group for just about everyone and everything. These intimate settings of community are the place where the real ministry of the church should take place as we study God's Word communally, while supporting and sharing our lives with one another.

There are several specific benefits for being a part of a small group. First, small groups are a place for believers to live together in community. The Christian faith is a social religion, not a solitary one, and God uses those around us to grow and shape who we are. Second, they are a place for believers to pray for one another. Prayer is one of God's greatest gifts that He has given the church and is the key to understanding and implementing the will of God. Third, small groups are a place to hear and learn from the Word of God through group study. Finally, small groups offer a place for disciples to be under the spiritual protection of godly leaders who will help them grow (see Hebrews 13:17; Acts 20:28–29). In today's culture that undervalues deep relationships, small groups offer a great blessing of being a part of a family of believers united by the same mission.

FAMILY DISCIPLESHIP

Finally, the call to make disciples begins in the home. While the church should offer a place of worship and discipleship, it should also equip families to grow outside the walls of the church. Faith is not just something that we do once a week, but it is something that should be a part of our daily lives. I fear that, for many families, the church is more like a baby-sitting service than a community for whole families. While church is important, the Bible tells us that the home is primary place of learning the Word and moral instruction. If we want a revolution of discipleship in our nation, our churches must empower families to own the call to discipleship. When this happens discipleship will spread organically through our neighborhoods and into the communities where we live. If every family in every church took seriously the call to make disciples in the home, our world would be turned upside down!

CONCLUSION

Growing people through intentional discipleship is essential for new churches from the very beginning if we are going to see ongoing multiplication of disciples. For many churches, the back door is as big as their front door, and they lose as many people as they gain. Over a long period of time, a new church will slowly die if it cannot close the back door and connect new people in deep and meaningful relationships with Christ and with others. Therefore, we need to be intentional about making disciples of Christ in our new churches through one-on-one, small group, and family forms of discipleship. To be effective, new churches must prioritize discipleship from the very beginning. As you think through what it will take for your church to reach its community, make sure the discipleship plan you develop lies at the very heart of your church's identity.

ESSENTIAL THOUGHT

Church planting is a revolutionary call for the church to return to a serious and intentional discipleship.

DISCUSSION QUESTIONS

1   Would you agree that there is a discipleship crisis in the Western world? Why do you answer the way you do? Discuss your reasoning.

2   Do you agree that many churches focus on evangelism at the expense of discipleship? If so, explain why and how that affects a church's ability to make disciples.

3   The most powerful paradigms for reproducing disciples are found in the discipleship methodology of Jesus. How can you implement the principles of *The Master Plan of Evangelism* into the way you make disciples?

4   Is discipleship intentional or unintentional? Or is it a little bit of both? Explain.

5   As disciples, why should we gather in small groups? Can't we just believe in Jesus and not be a part of His church?

ACTION ITEMS

Think and pray about one or two people with whom you can begin a one-on-one discipleship relationship.

Write an intentional discipleship plan for your new church that addresses how people can be a part of one-on-one discipleship, small groups, and family discipleship.

CHURCH
PLANT
PROFILE

— — — — — — — — — — — —

Planters: **Graham and Céline Singh**
Type: **Replant**
Church: **St. James**
Location: **Montréal, Canada**

— — — — — — — — — — — —

Graham Singh isn't your typical church planter. Graham seeks to restore the heart of cities by replanting churches in historic, yet abandoned church buildings. Graham says, "An empty building in a city is to the city like the empty palace of a long forgotten king."[1] With more than one thousand churches likely closing in the next five years, Graham has a heart for the buildings and the hope their restoration symbolizes, not only to the brick-and-mortar structures, but also to the communities.

In 2016, Graham and Céline Singh and a growing team of volunteers reopened doors of the historic 150-plus-year-old Church of St. James the Apostle on Rue Sainte-Catherine in the heart of downtown Montréal, which is one of the most unchurched cities in the Western Hemisphere.

The church had died and closed its doors, but now breathes with new life! After spending months reaching out to the community, Graham and his teams reopened the doors of the historic St. James on Easter Sunday 2016 with nearly one hundred people at their opening service. Their services are in both English and French so they are able to reach across ethnic boundaries.

Graham has drawn his inspiration for discipleship from the Alpha Course. Alpha is an evangelistic program that is a ten-week course including a meal, short talk, and time for questions that is designed to bring unchurched people into the church. By employing the Alpha model in both French and English, St. James is able to continuously reach out to those in the diverse area of Montréal.

Graham describes the vision of the church in the following way:

> Imagine an exciting, new community of faith in Jesus Christ, right in the heart of downtown Montréal; a church with vibrant worship in English and French where bilingual families and individuals can celebrate God's love, together; a church home where children are an integral part of every gathering, inspired by their parents and grandparents to grow in their faith.[2]

St. James is an example of how dying churches can be resurrected and bring new life into old buildings. For more information about Graham and Céline Singh and St. James, visit **http://stjax.org**.

CHAPTER SIX

AN ORGANIC PROCESS

*The goal is just enough structure to provide a way
forward without squelching Spirit-led adaptability.*
—Travis Collins

At this point, you may be wondering, *What is the actual process
of starting a new church?* While the context of church planting
is very different from place to place, there is an organic process
of church planting that is applicable to a variety of different
contexts.

You may be asking yourself the question, *Why organic?*
The answer is in the Bible. The New Testament is based on
an organic view of the church and uses various metaphors
to describe spiritual growth such as sowing and reaping
(see John 4:37; 2 Corinthians 9:6), planting and watering (see
1 Corinthians 3:6), growing (see 1 Peter 2:2; 2 Peter 3:18),
and bearing fruit (see Matthew 7:17–20; John 15:1–16;
Galatians 5:22). In addition, the church is spoken of as a family
(e.g., the use of terms such as *brother, sister, mother, father,
bride,* etc.) and the body of Christ. The church is the spiritual and living body of Christ. Like all healthy organisms, it

Phases to Church Planting

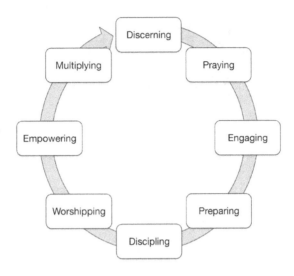

requires numerous systems and structures that work together to fulfill its intended purpose and overall health. Just as the physical body has to have an organic structure to hold it together while allowing it to grow and develop, likewise the body of Christ must have an organic structure that can do the same. As a new church continues to grow and change, it will outgrow its old systems and structures. Thus, in the words of Leonard Sweet, "We must develop ministries that continually adjust and change with our continually changing culture."[3]

An organic approach to church planting offers enough structure to maintain order, but is flexible enough to change with the ongoing needs of the church as it grows. An organic understanding of church planting will require church leaders to rethink current church systems and structures in biblical terms. In this chapter, I want to explore the tenets of organic church planting. The following eight phases for starting new churches are what I believe to be the foundation of such an approach.

EIGHT PHASES TO CHURCH PLANTING

1. DISCERNING: HEARING GOD'S CALL

Church planting begins with a clear sense of hearing God's call. Any other motivation, no matter how good it may be, is not enough. Therefore, it is essential that before anyone begins planting a new church they must hear God's call. In Acts 16:9, we are told that "During the night Paul had a vision of a man of Macedonia standing and begging him, 'Come over to Macedonia and help us'" (NIV). Immediately afterward, Paul redirected his steps and left to establish the church at Philippi. In the same way, we must also hear God's voice to receive assurance of His calling to church planting.

Here are a couple of thoughts for hearing God's voice. First, pray for God's voice and direction in church planting. He may speak through a still, small voice in your heart in prayer. A lot of people see prayer as a monologue rather than a dialogue. Don't just talk to God; stop and let Him talk to you. Be patient and listen. Second, God speaks through ordinary everyday events and circumstances. Never underestimate small things that happen from day-to-day to confirm His calling, because the Lord may be using them to speak to you. Last, God might use somebody else to speak to you, even when you least expect it. Sometimes God may use someone you already know; other times He may use a complete stranger. The Bible is full of stories and examples of how God speaks through others to share His Word. Don't be afraid to ask God for direction in your life. He speaks to those who are willing to ask and listen.

2. PRAYING: BUILDING A PRAYER TEAM

For Christians, every new endeavor must begin in prayer. Therefore, intercessory prayer is essential to the foundation of starting a new church. According to Webster, to *intercede* means simply, "to go or pass between; to act between parties with a view to reconcile those who differ or contend; to interpose; to mediate or make intercession; mediation." If you are going to be planting a church, you will need an intercessory prayer team to bathe it in prayer from the very beginning. Start praying now! As you move forward, gather an intercessory prayer team to pray for you, the new church, and the community in which you feel called to plant. Identify people who have a passion for prayer to lead this vital ministry.

There are various ways that you can seek to integrate prayer into the life of your church plant. First, make prayer a priority in everything that you do from the beginning. Start with a prayer ministry that can saturate your church plant and the community you serve in prayer. Establish prayer teams to pray confidentially with people. Start a prayer chain of people to regularly pray for you, your church, and the needs in your community. Last, pray that God will give you the right opportunity and words to say to others as you reach out into the community. These are just a few ways to ensure that all that you do as a church proceeds in a manner that seeks to serve the will of God.

3. ENGAGING: GETTING TO KNOW YOUR COMMUNITY

Holistic church planting happens by getting to know the community and context where you feel called to start a new church. It begins by recognizing the needs in your community and getting to know the people God is calling you to reach. What is unique about the culture and context of your city? Who are the people that you will reach? Who are these people? Where do they live? Where can we find them? They are not numbers or mere statistics, but they have names, faces, and feelings. More important, they have real needs that can be helped by the church. You will never know what the needs of your community are until you begin to get outside of the four walls of the church and get into the community. It is amazing how little Christians actually interact with non-churchgoers, especially people from different ethnic and socioeconomic backgrounds.

Matthew 9:36 tells us that when Jesus went out into all the cities and villages, He saw that the multitudes were weary and had compassion on them. As Jesus went into the community, He saw the needs of the people. Likewise, when you get into the community, you will begin to see what the needs of the people are. When you begin to canvass the city and assess these needs, you will see many people with tremendous wounds all around you. Get to know your unchurched neighbors and their families. Find out their interests and their passions.

As you become an intimate witness to the people around you, make a personal inventory of the needs, and then you will be able to guide your new church's mission in a way that meets the needs of your community. There are a number of ways that you can do effective community ministry that is missional. Depending upon the need in your community, your church can start an art ministry to reach local artists, start a food pantry, serve meals to the elderly, offer literacy training, or start an after-school program for at-risk youth. Community ministry shows people in the community that you care. Use the demographic worksheet in the back of the book to help you understand and know more about the community where you feel called to start a new church.

4. PREPARING: DEVELOPING A STRATEGIC PLAN

Now that you have prayed and begun to get to know your community, the next step is to develop a strategic plan. Church planting doesn't just happen; it is the result of a planned process. Therefore, developing a strategic plan is essential to starting a new church. In Luke 14:28–30, we find Jesus speaking about the importance of planning. He says, "Suppose one of you wants to build a tower. Won't you first sit down and estimate the cost to see if you have enough money to complete it? For if you lay the foundation and are not able to finish it, everyone who sees it will ridicule you, saying, 'This person began to build and wasn't able to finish'" (NIV).

Jesus' words are especially applicable to those who feel that God has called them to plant a church. We must count the cost before starting a new church. Many church planters write a church-planting proposal that helps guide the direction of the new work and helps others understand the vision. Such a plan answers questions like: Why start a new church? Who is this church going to reach? What kind of church are we going to plant? How and when will we plant this church? What will make this church different? What is God asking this new church to do? Developing a plan that answers these and other questions will help you accomplish the vision of starting a new church. Use the strategic plan in the back of the book to help you and your team prayerfully think through the next steps of the church-planting process.

5. DISCIPLING: MAKING AND MATURING DISCIPLES

New churches play an important role in our spiritual growth and development as disciples and followers of Jesus Christ. While modern models may tend to value quantity, these churches should not simply be concerned with growing numbers, but with growing members through discipleship. Spiritual growth and discipleship happen in a number of ways through the local church. However, one of the primary ways the church makes disciples is by providing a place for people to hear, learn, and study the Word of God within the context of Christian community under godly leadership.

New churches can become a school of Christ that helps people become disciples and grow in their faith in a variety of ways. New churches can offer training and small groups that help Christians grow and learn to apply the Bible to everyday life. When I was a new believer, my church helped me learn to read my Bible and encouraged me to pray and to share my faith with others. Learning about God's Word within the context of a new church allows people to ask important questions, dialogue, and learn from other believers who have more wisdom and experience.

6. WORSHIPPING: GATHERING TOGETHER IN WORSHIP

A new church is birthed as people begin to come together to worship, pray, and learn God's Word. In its earliest expression, the church meant a group of individuals who had come together to worship in the name of Jesus Christ. As we have already seen, the church is not the building, but the people who come together to worship and serve God. This doesn't have to be in a traditional church building, but can take place in a living room, coffee bar, school cafeteria, or under a tree.

As Christians, we don't just gather to stay together, but to be prepared to go back out into the world in mission. The worship gathering actually feeds us and prepares us to be missionaries to the world in which God has called us to live. Theologian N. T. Wright described this connection in the following way: "The link between worship and mission is so close that many prefer to speak of them in terms of each other. Glad, rich worship of the God revealed in Jesus invites outsiders to come in, welcomes them, nourishes them, and challenges them."[4] The God we worship when we gather invites others into the worshipping community of the church. Therefore, a new church is a gathering of believers who come together to worship God and then are sent back out into the world on mission to invite others to come and join in worship.

7. EMPOWERING: RELEASING SERVANT LEADERS

New churches should seek to inspire a servant revolution by developing leaders from the very beginning of the plant. While modern models may tend to value quantity, new multiplying churches should not simply be concerned with growing numbers, but with growing servant leaders. But where do we even begin to do this? This whole process starts with empowering and releasing disciples to serve God and others.

Service is foundational to being a Christian. By recovering Christian service and providing opportunities for those around you to put others before themselves, you can create a culture that values serving. An organic process should find ways to help people grow as disciples by using their gifts and talents for God in a way that will bless others and make the community a better place. By using the gifts that the Holy Spirit gives, believers grow and mature in their faith. As a church, we must find ways to recognize the gifts of the congregation and empower them to put these gifts into action.

Unfortunately, our individualistic society has caused us to neglect the need for putting others above ourselves. For our culture, serving is revolutionary because it goes against the natural tendency toward self-preservation and elevation. Service calls us to selflessness as opposed to selfishness. The mind of a servant constantly looks around and asks, "What can I do for others" instead of "What can they do for me?" We find this mind-set pervading the life of Jesus. He set the ultimate example by living out this mantra: "the Son of Man did not come to be served, but to serve, and to give his life as a ransom for many" (Mark 10:45 NIV). As disciples of the greatest teacher, Christians must strive to be like Jesus, our perfect example. By engaging in faithful servanthood, we, as the body of Christ, become Christ's representatives to a lost world.

As a whole, the church should be an army of servants who are making a positive difference in their families, community, and the world. As you lead your church in discipleship, find creative pathways for people to connect to your church through serving. With a commitment to servant leadership, we are bound to witness a revolution that will transform our community and demonstrate the love of Christ for the world to see!

8. MULTIPLYING: CHURCHES PLANTING CHURCHES

Finally, don't just plant a church, but plant a movement. Begin with a vision to multiply everything, including disciples, small groups, and more churches. From the very beginning, cast the vision to be a multiplying church that makes disciples and plants more churches. There is no happier time than when a family is getting ready to have a baby. Sadly, many Christians and new churches will never reproduce themselves. The result is that they take their faith and legacy with them to the grave. And nearly 80 percent of all evangelical churches in the United States have either stopped growing or are in decline! What does this mean? Simple: the church in North America is not multiplying. As you consider church planting, why not plant a reproducing, disciple-making church that multiplies itself by planting more churches? We don't just need one more church, we need churches that will be multiplying church-planting churches.

Throughout this book you have seen how every church is different and that no cookie-cutter approach to church planting will succeed for everyone. However, in spite of this diversity, we see that successful churches do embrace key common tenets that are foundational to the success of every plant. What we see is that the process of planting a church is organic. It begins with hearing the call from the Lord and then proceeds by getting to know the community, and building relationships with the lost and unchurched. The goal of this entire process is to make disciples of Christ and bring them together in a worshipping community, and teaching them to multiply. As you start your church and implement these core values, don't stop! You must continually implement these foundations and create a culture of multiplication. By planting churches that plant new churches, we can better ensure that the legacy of a congregation will live long beyond its founding stages.

ESSENTIAL THOUGHT

While the context of church planting is very different from place to place, there is a general pattern to the process of church planting.

DISCUSSION QUESTIONS

1   What is the general process of starting a new church that was discussed in this chapter?

2   How might that be different in your setting or context?

3   What would you add or take away from the list?

4   Why do you think that it is important to develop a plan for starting a new church?

5   Based on this chapter, what are some of the most important things that you think are necessary in preparing to start a new church?

ACTION ITEMS

Begin meeting with a small group of people who are interested in starting a new church to pray and talk about the possibilities.

Hold an informational meeting for those who are interested in starting a new church in your community to share the vision and ask for feedback.

CHURCH PLANT PROFILE

Planters:	**Kevin and Grace Haah**
Type:	**Multiethnic**
Church:	**New City Church**
Location:	**Los Angeles, CA**

Kevin Haah never dreamed of being a church planter. He used to practice law before he received a life-changing phone call one day. Kevin recalls,

> I got a phone call from an anonymous caller who ultimately asked me, "What are you doing to reach out to all of the new residents of downtown LA?" We had a polite conversation, but, for some reason this question started to resonate in my soul. I began asking myself the same question. Until then, I had never seriously considered what was going on in downtown LA.[1]

Soon afterward, Kevin began to dream about planting a multiethnic, multi-socioeconomic church in downtown that would reach out to both the Skid Row residents and the new loft dwellers.

Then, in 2008, Kevin and Grace Haah stepped out in faith and planted New City Church with a bold vision to create a church that embraces diversity in downtown Los Angeles, California. After only a few years, the church has grown to fulfill their vision and is now a fellowship of people from across Los Angeles. According to their website,

> New City Church of Los Angeles is a multi-ethnic, multi-socioeconomic Christian church in downtown LA. We are a diverse and inclusive community seeking to be like Jesus. We have roughly equal numbers of Blacks, Whites, Asians, and Latinos; about a third of us come from Skid Row, and the rest come from downtown lofts and outside of downtown; we are families, singles, and kids, Democrats and Republicans, gay and straight, poor and rich, moral and loose.[2]

Today Kevin also leads the LA Church Planting Movement, a network working with the national church-planting organization, Stadia, to plant churches in 119 Los Angeles neighborhoods. Kevin and his wife, Grace, are an amazing example of what God can do with someone who is willing to step out in faith and dream of starting a new kind of church that reaches people from different ethnic and socio-economic backgrounds with the love of Jesus. For more information on Kevin and Grace Haah and New City Church, visit **http://newcitychurchla.com.**

NEXT STEPS

For many of us, C. S. Lewis's *The Lion, the Witch and the Wardrobe* represents a classic story from our childhood. There is something about this story of four children named Lucy, Susan, Peter, and Edmond traveling through the magical kingdom of Narnia that forces us to reflect on the journey of our own lives. For those of you who haven't read these classics (you are really missing out if you haven't!), Lewis wrote this story as an allegory of Jesus Christ and his kingdom, with Christ represented as a lion named Aslan. At one point in Narnia, the children meet Mr. and Mrs. Beaver, and when they ask the beavers to describe Aslan, they are astonished by what they hear:

"Is—is he a man?" asked Lucy.

"Aslan a man!" said Mr. Beaver sternly. "Certainly not. I tell you he is the King of the wood and the son of the great Emperor-Beyond-the-Sea. Don't you know who is the King of Beasts? Aslan is a lion—the lion, the great Lion."

"Ooh!" said Susan, "I'd thought he was a man. Is he—quite safe? I shall feel rather nervous about meeting a lion."

"That you will, dearie, and no mistake," said Mrs. Beaver; "if there's anyone who can appear before Aslan without their knees knocking, they're either braver than most or else just silly."

"Then he isn't safe?" said Lucy.

"Safe?" said Mr. Beaver; "don't you hear what Mrs. Beaver tells you? Who said anything about safe? 'Course he isn't safe. But he's good. He's the King, I tell you."[3]

Is church planting safe? The answer is no. Revolutionary movements are never safe as they are often unpredictable, unstable, and uncontrollable. If you can control it, then it is not a revolution. Church planting isn't safe, but neither is being a disciple of Christ. When Christ calls, we are required to give an answer. We cannot simply ignore it or leave it unanswered. Either we will trust and obey, or doubtfully deny. If we want to follow him, our yes must mean that we lay down everything we have for the sake of the gospel. As Dietrich Bonhoeffer said, "When Christ calls a man, he bids him come and die."[4] In this sense, it is a call to total self-surrender. Two thousand years later, we are still expected to leave everything to follow Jesus, just as the disciples did in their day.

The church-planting revolution isn't safe, but it's good! It is a response to the radical call of discipleship. It is not for the faint of heart, but for brave souls who are tired of just attending church and are longing to join in the Jesus movement to make and multiply disciples.

So if you are sensing this call, I have one question: Why not join the church-planting revolution? God is using the most unlikely men and women to plant new contextualized churches in the most unlikely of ways in the most unlikely of places. If, after reading this, you sense God calling you to be a part of starting a new church, I would like to offer a few next steps for your church-planting journey.

First, if you feel called to be the lead planter, I would highly recommend taking the Church-Planting EQ Assessment test before setting a plan into action. Assessments come in a variety of formats and they help provide potential planters with an initial indicator of their readiness to plant a church. By evaluating different characteristics that are important for potential church planters, these tests offer a valuable lens through which you can evaluate yourself. While there are no magical assessments that automatically guarantee that you will succeed as a church planter, a good assessment will help you get a better handle on your potential calling to the ministry of church planting. Go to the website found on page 117 to take the Church-Planting EQ Assessment.

Another next step to consider is pursuing church-planting training. There are many different ways to be trained for church planting, from informal workshops to graduate degree programs. Seedbed and New Room offer additional training and resources for church planters, and institutions like Asbury Seminary are committed to equipping church leaders through innovative training programs that are theologically grounded to help anchor the growth of church-planting endeavors around the world. Whether it be informal or formal, training will function as the foundation of your pursuit of God's calling.

As you are praying about starting a new church, I would recommend finding a coach and a mentor who can help you discern your calling to church planting. Everybody needs a coach, a mentor, a "Gandalf." Many seasoned church planters love to share their ministry experiences with a church planter who is beginning his or her ministry journey, and these people can provide tremendous insight as you undertake your journey. There are a number of professional church-planting coaches that come alongside those who are planting for the first time. I would strongly suggest finding a coach as you continue to pursue church planting. Along these lines, it is important to be a part of a denomination, network, or tribe for support and encouragement. Church planting can be a lonely business, and having others come alongside you can help ensure your success.

Throughout the book, I have mentioned the importance of planning when it comes to church planting. As you are thinking and praying through next steps, utilize the tools and worksheets in the back of the book to help you work through the next steps of developing a strategic plan for starting a new church. Strategic planning is an essential step for you and your team to take together as you dream together about starting a new church that is unique for your community and context.

Connected to strategic planning is getting to know your community. Use the demographic worksheet in appendix B to help you effectively understand the context where you are planning to plant a church. In order to be most effective, you must know the cultural identity of the community where your church is located, and this worksheet is a great resource for thinking about how to reach those around you.

Last, if you are confident that God has called you to be a part of church planting, then step out in faith. Church planting is an apostolic venture of faith that begins with taking the first step. Just like Abraham, step out in faith and go where the Lord has called you to go. Put your life in His hands and be willing to pursue the call of God to start a new church. If God has really called you and your team to plant a church, He will make a way. Hold on to the call of the Lord and know that He is with you and will never leave you or forsake you. There is a place for you in this exciting new world of church planting, and God is waiting for you to respond and go!

APPENDICES

STRATEGIC PLANNING GUIDE

FIVE BIG QUESTIONS

Every new church should start with a detailed, written strategic plan to help guide them through the process of church planting. A strategic plan is not a straitjacket, but a plan that can allow the Holy Spirit to guide you as you prepare to plant a new church. The following is an outline for a written church-planting strategic plan that can help guide you and your church-planting team. Think through each section. Create a written description for each item and compile them in the following order.

1. WHY START A NEW CHURCH?

> Describe your calling to church planting
> Describe what kind of church you are planting
> Demonstrate the need for the new church
> Explain what your role will be in the new church

2. WHAT KIND OF CHURCH WILL IT BE?

> Write your vision/mission statement
> List your core values

5 Big Questions

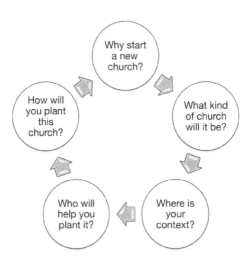

> Describe your church-planting model
> Describe your plan for discipleship
> Describe how the church will be governed

3. WHERE IS YOUR CONTEXT?

> Describe your target people group
> Describe the community needs
> Describe the appropriate demographics
> Describe the location of the new church

4. WHO WILL HELP YOU PLANT IT?

> Describe key ministry teams that will be needed
> List the team members you will need

> Include a list of potential ministry partners
> List the name of ten to twelve intercessors who will pray

5. HOW WILL YOU PLANT THIS CHURCH?

> Include a detailed time line for the first twelve to thirty-six months
> Include a detailed list of things you must accomplish
> Include a start-up budget and describe your funding strategy
> Include salary for any paid staff
> List potential financial supporters (one time, monthly, annually)

DEMOGRAPHIC WORKSHEET

Getting to know your context of ministry is an essential part of strategic planning for church planting. The purpose of this worksheet is to collect information about the people living in your target area so you can gain a general insight into who they are before you plant. Fill in as much of the information for your area as you can by using one of the recommended free demographic resources listed here. These reports contain all the information plus much more.

Gathering demographic research can be overwhelming if we don't know what to do with the information that we have gathered about the location in which we are seeking to start a new church. So what do we do with the demographic information? According to Craig Ott and Gene Wilson, authors of *Global Church Planting*, there are four things that they recommend when doing demographic research: data collection, data analysis, application to strategy, and evaluation.[1] After you have filled out the demographic information, answer the following four questions.

1. DATA COLLECTION
> What is the demographic information?

2. DATA ANALYSIS
> *What does this information tell us about the community and the people?*

3. APPLICATION TO STRATEGY
> *What do we need to do based on this information?*

4. EVALUATION
> *How do we implement a plan based on this information?*

FREE DEMOGRAPHIC RESOURCES
http://factfinder.census.gov
http://www.peoplegroups.info
http://www.freedemographics.com

DESCRIPTION	NEW CHURCH AREA	LOCAL TREND (+ OR -)	NATIONAL AVERAGE
Average Age			
Median Age			
% Population under 18			
% Population 18–24			
% Population 25–34			
% Population 35–44			
% Population 45–54			
% Population over 55			
% Females			
% Males			
Average Household Income			

Median Household Income			
% Blue-Collar Workers			
% White-Collar Workers			
Average Number of Kids Per Family			
Average Home Price			
% People Owning Their Home vs. Renting			
% White			
% Black			
% Asian			
% Hispanic			
% over 16, Unemployed			
% over 16, Not in Work Force			
% Single-Parent Homes			
% Adults Married			
% over 16, Never Married			
% Divorced			
% Head of Household with College Degree			
% over 25, No College Experience			
% Commuting Outside Local Area to Work			
Average Drive Time to Work (Estimate if data not available)			

APPENDIX C

CHURCH-PLANTING EQ ASSESSMENT

Our world is inundated with online surveys and personality profile tests that evaluate everything from leadership capacity to emotional intelligence. My family and I recently took a modern version of the Myers-Briggs personality tool called "16 Personalities." This particular website boasts, "Take our Personality Test and get a 'freakishly accurate' description of who you are and why you do things the way you do." To our amazement, it accurately identified each member of our family, including our ten-year-old daughter! The test identified her as an ENTJ, which are "Bold, imaginative and strong-willed leaders, always finding a way—or making one." If you knew my daughter Anna Belle, you would know that this is a very accurate assessment of her personality. You should try taking one of these assessments at some point just to see the results! For example, see https://www.16personalities.com/free-personality-test.

Regarding church planting, there are a variety of personal assessments that are designed to help assess your readiness. Assessments come in a variety of formats and they help provide potential planters with an initial indicator of their readiness to plant a church. By evaluating different characteristics that are important for potential church planters, these tests offer a valuable lens through which you can evaluate yourself. As you continue to explore the exciting new world of church planting, I would highly recommend taking a church planter assessment test, especially if you plan to be a full-time church planter with funding. Taking an assessment allows you to have tangible evidence of your skill set and calling into this field.

A church planter assessment presents a thorough and comprehensive process for the evaluation and assessment of potential church planters and it is essential to a strategy for planting healthy churches. It would be presumptuous, to say the least, to claim that any assessment could proclaim who God can and cannot use to plant a church. Rather, the assessment process is meant to facilitate the discernment of the church as to the readiness of a candidate with regard to the skills, knowledge, and fitness that are needed for the task of planting.

WHAT IS EQ?

I have chosen the EQ model because I believe it to be the best method of creating meaningful reflection. EQ does not refer to our IQ, but is another "kind of smart": our emotional intelligence. This emotional intelligence (EI), or emotional quotient (EQ), reflects the capability of individuals to recognize and use their own emotional information to manage and adapt to various environments in order to achieve success. Rather than focusing on your ability to perform tasks, EQ probes the depths of identity to ensure that at your very core, you possess the character, stamina, and adaptability to succeed as a church planter. In the words of Drs. Travis Bradberry and Jean Greaves, "Emotional intelligence is your ability to recognize and understand emotions in yourself and others, and your ability to use this awareness to manage your behavior and relationships."[1] They believe that emotional intelligence affects how we manage behavior, navigate social complexities, and make personal decisions that achieve positive results. According to Bradberry and Greaves, emotional intelligence is made up of four core skills that pair up under two primary competencies: personal competence and social competence.

I believe that there are similar personal and social competencies for church planters. After working with hundreds of church planters for more than a decade, I have helped create an assessment tool to test the EQ of potential church planters. I have designed the Church Planter EQ Assessment to answer the question, "Do I have the emotional intelligence to be a church planter?" The assessment helps give a "snapshot" of your life and ministry experiences in order to help you discover your readiness for church planting.

Dozens of people have taken the assessment and found it to be a helpful tool as they contemplated their calling to church planting. In the words of one person who recently took the assessment, "The assessment tool was useful to me in identifying areas in which I am strong and confident and then areas I may need to be more committed and devoted to improving. I enjoyed taking this assessment and identifying areas that I needed to improve in and I also feel it affirmed my calling to church planting."

Through research and evaluation, I have identified eight key factors that are important for individuals to take into consideration when they are evaluating their readiness for starting a new church. The eight factors can be divided into two categories: personal competence and social competence. While there are no magical assessments that automatically guarantee success, this guide is intended to be an initial self-assessment tool that will help you gain a more well-rounded understanding of your potential calling to and readiness for the ministry of church planting.

EIGHT FACTORS

1. PERSONAL COMPETENCE

Personal: Being emotionally, physically, and financially healthy
Spiritual: Having a vibrant walk with Christ and daily devotional life
Vocational: Having a clear sense of calling
Visional: Seeing a preferred future beyond the present

2. SOCIAL COMPETENCE

Relational: Maintaining healthy and supportive relationships
Cultural: Understanding culture and context
Missional: Building relationships with unchurched people
Adaptable: Being flexible and adaptable to changes and needs

TAKE THE ASSESSMENT

Visit www.churchplantingeq.com to take the Church-Planting EQ Assessment to help create a snapshot of your life and ministry experiences and to help you discover your readiness for church planting.

NOTES

INTRODUCTION

1. For a fuller explanation see Michael Frost and Alan Hirsch, *The Shaping of Things to Come: Innovation and Movement for the 21st-Century Church* (Peabody, MA: Hendrickson, 2003), 8.
2. Ibid.
3. See Ed Stetzer and David Putman, *Breaking the Missional Code: Your Church Can Become a Missionary in Your Community* (Nashville, TN: Broadman & Holman: 2006), 48.

CHURCH PLANTER PROFILE AND CHAPTER 1

1. See http://asburyseminary.edu/voices/matt-leroy/.
2. Ibid.
3. Ed Stetzer, *Planting Missional Churches: Planting a Church That's Biblically Sound and Reaching People in Culture* (Nashville, TN: Broadman & Holman 2006), 19.
4. Christopher J. H. Wright, *The Mission of God: Unlocking the Bible's Grand Narrative* (Downers Grove, IL: InterVarsity, 2006), 62.
5. Tim Chester and Steve Timmis, *Total Church: A Radical Reshaping around Gospel and Community* (Wheaton, IL: Crossway, 2008), 85.
6. For a more detailed discussion, see Dr. Timothy Tennent's examination of the statistics regarding unreached people groups in *Invitation to World Missions: A Trinitarian Missiology for the Twenty-First Century* (Grand Rapids, MI: Kregel Publications, 2010), 360. Here, he explores resources from three major missionary organizations: International Mission Board (IMB), the Joshua Project, and the World Christian Database.
7. John Stott, *Christian Mission in the Modern World* (Downers Grove, IL: InterVarsity, 1975), n.p.
8. Alvin L. Reid, *Radically Unchurched: Who They Are & How to Reach Them* (Grand Rapids, MI: Kregel Publications, 2002), 21.
9. George G. Hunter III, *The Recovery of a Contagious Methodist Movement* (Nashville, TN: Abingdon Press, 2011), 28.
10. Leonard I. Sweet, *Soul Tsunami: Sink or Swim in the New Millennium Culture* (Grand Rapids, MI: Zondervan, 1999), 17.
11. Millard Erickson, *Postmodernizing the Faith: Evangelical Responses to the Challenge of Postmodernism* (Grand Rapids, MI: Baker, 1998), 19.
12. C. Peter Wagner, *Church Planting for a Greater Harvest: A Comprehensive Guide* (Ventura, CA: Regal Books, 1990), 11.

13. Ed Stetzer and Daniel Im, *Planting Missional Churches: Your Guide to Starting Churches That Multiply* (Nashville, TN: Broadman & Holeman, 2016), 8.
14. Win Arn, cited in Ed Stetzer, *Planting New Churches in a Postmodern Age* (Nashville, TN: Broadman & Holman, 2003), 10.
15. David T. Olson, *The American Church in Crisis: Groundbreaking Research Based on a National Database of over 200,000 Churches* (Grand Rapids, MI: Zondervan, 2008), 29.
16. Stetzer and Im, *Planting Missional Churches*, 7.
17. Chester and Timmis, *Total Church*, 96.
18. See Neil Cole, *Organic Church: Growing Faith Where Life Happens* (San Francisco, CA: Jossey-Bass, 2005).

CHURCH PLANTER PROFILE AND CHAPTER 2

1. See http://kxc.org.uk.
2. Ibid.
3. Ibid.
4. Ed Stetzer, *Planting New Churches in a Postmodern Age* (Nashville, TN: Broadman & Holman, 2003), 35.
5. Michael Moynagh, *Church for Every Context: An Introduction to Theology and Practice* (London, England: SCM Press, 2012), 194.
6. Aubrey Malphurs, *Planting Growing Churches for the 21st Century: A Comprehensive Guide for New Churches and Those Desiring Renewal* (Grand Rapids, MI: Baker Books, 1998), 21.
7. See "Bishop of Islington Consecrated at St. Paul's Cathedral," Diocese of London, September 29, 2015, http://www.london.anglican.org/articles/bishop -of-islington-ric-thorpe-consecrated-st-pauls-cathedral/.

CHURCH PLANTER PROFILE AND CHAPTER 3

1. See http://www.ministrymatters.com/all/entry/3437/learning-to-love-the-church.
2. Neil Cole, *Organic Church: Growing Faith Where Life Happens* (San Francisco, CA: Jossey-Bass, 2005), xxix.
3. See "Mike Breen: What Is a Missional Community?" Verge, December 31, 2010, http://www.vergenetwork.org/2010/12/31/mike-breen-what-is-a-missional -community-printable/.
4. See http://asburyseminary.edu/voices/bryan-collier/.
5. Martin Robinson, *Planting Mission-Shaped Churches Today* (Oxford, UK: Monarch Books, 2006), 144.
6. See http://asburyseminary.edu/voices/anderson-moyo/.
7. This definition is from the Fresh Expressions UK website https://www.fresh expressions.org.uk.
8. See https://www.freshexpressions.org.uk/about/whatis.
9. Travis Collins, *Fresh Expressions of Church* (Franklin, TN: Seedbed Publishing, 2015), 42.
10. See http://www.grahamsingh.org/news/dead-alive-church.
11. Francis A. Schaeffer, *Escape from Reason: A Penetrating Analysis of Trends in Modern Thought* (Downers Grove, IL: InterVarsity Press, 1968), 11–12.

CHURCH PLANTER PROFILE AND CHAPTER 4

1. See http://asburyseminary.edu/voices/luke-edwards/.
2. In particular, I have drawn from the work of Roland Allen's *Spontaneous Expansion of the Church*, David Garrison's *Church Planting Movements*, George G. Hunter's *The Recovery of a Contagious Methodist Movement*, and Steve Addison's *Movements That Change the World*. I have also drawn inspiration and wisdom for twenty-first-century church planting from insights from the eighteenth-century Wesleyan revival, which I believe offers a model for missional church planting in the twenty-first century.
3. For more information on the growth of Methodism see C. C. Goss's book, *The Statistical History of the First Century of American Methodism* (New York: Carlton & Porter, 1866) and Roger Finke and Rodney Stark, *The Churching of America, 1776–2005: Winners and Losers in Our Religious Economy* (Piscataway, NJ: Rutgers University Press, 2005), 55 ff.
4. George G. Hunter III, *The Recovery of a Contagious Methodist Movement* (Nashville, TN: Abingdon Press, 2011), 5.
5. Steve Addison, *Movements That Change the World: Five Keys to Spreading the Gospel* (Downers Grove, IL: InterVarsity Press, 2011), 37.
6. Quoted in John Telford's *The Life of John Wesley* (London: Hodder & Stoughton, 1886), accessed through the Wesley Center for Applied Theology at Northwest Nazarene University. http://wesley.nnu.edu/john-wesley/the-life-of-john -wesley-by-john-telford/the-life-of-john-wesley-by-john-telford-chapter-14.
7. John Telford, *The Life of John Wesley* (London: The Epworth Press, 1947), 394.
8. See http://wesley.nnu.edu/john-wesley/the-letters-of-john-wesley/wesleys -letters-1777.
9. David Garrison, *Church Planting Movements: How God Is Redeeming a Lost World* (Monument, CO: WIG Take Resources, 2004), 189.
10. Albert C. Outler, *John Wesley* (New York: Oxford University Press, 1964; 1980), 178. See also Kevin M. Watson's *The Class Meeting: Reclaiming a Forgotten (and Essential) Small Group Experience* (Franklin, TN: Seedbed, 2014).
11. *The Works of John Wesley*, 5:187. See also Andrew C. Thompson, *The Means of Grace: Traditioned Practice in Today's World* (Franklin, TN: Seedbed Publishing, 2015).
12. Emil Brunner quoted in Michael Griffiths, *God's Forgetful Pilgrims: Recalling the Church to Its Reason for Being* (Grand Rapids, MI: Wm. B. Eerdmans Publishing Co., 1975), 135.
13. *The Rule of St. Benedict* (Collegeville, MN: The Liturgical Press, 1982), 73.

CHURCH PLANTER PROFILE AND CHAPTER 5

1. See http://asburyseminary.edu/voices/carolyn-moore/.
2. Ibid.
3. John R. W. Stott, "Make Disciples, Not Just Converts: Evangelism without Discipleship Dispenses Cheap Grace," *Christianity Today*, Vol. 43, No. 12 (October 25, 1999): 28.
4. Stanley Grenz, *Theology for the Community of God* (Grand Rapids, MI: Wm B. Eerdmans Publishing Co., 2000), 504.

5. Dallas Willard, *The Divine Conspiracy: Rediscovering Our Hidden Life in God* (New York: HarperCollins, 1998), 304.
6. Ibid., 68.
7. Alan Hirsch, *The Forgotten Ways: Reactivating the Missional Church* (Grand Rapids, MI: Brazos Press, 2006), 45.
8. Ibid., 55.
9. This conclusion is based upon two years of research Barna conducted regarding the current state of discipleship, and how churches might enhance the effectiveness of their discipleship ministries. See George Barna, *Growing True Disciples: New Strategies for Producing Genuine Followers of Christ* (Colorado Springs, CO: WaterBrook Press, 2001).
10. Dallas Willard, "Rethinking Evangelism," *Cutting Edge Magazine*, Vol. 5, No. 1 (Winter 2001).
11. Robert E. Coleman, *The Master Plan of Evangelism* (Grand Rapids, MI: Revell, 1963; 2010), 21.

CHURCH PLANTER PROFILE AND CHAPTER 6

1. See http://stjax.org/ourvision/.
2. Ibid.
3. Leonard Sweet, *Aqua Church* (Loveland, CO: Group, 1999), 8.
4. Marcus Borg and N. T. Wright, *The Meaning of Jesus: Two Visions* (San Francisco, CA: HarperCollins, 1999), 207.

CHURCH PLANTER PROFILE AND EPILOGUE

1. See http://newcitychurchla.com.
2. Ibid.
3. C. S. Lewis, *The Lion, the Witch and the Wardrobe* (New York, NY: Harper Collins, 1950), 79–80.
4. Dietrich Bonhoeffer, *The Cost of Discipleship* (New York: Touchstone, 1995), 89.

APPENDIX B

1. Craig Ott and Gene Wilson, *Global Church Planting* (Grand Rapids, MI: Baker Academics, 2011), 192.

APPENDIX C

1. Travis Bradberry and Jean Greaves, *Emotional Intelligence 2.0* (San Diego, CA: TalentSmart, 2009), 17.

ABOUT THE EXPONENTIAL SERIES

Interest in church planting has grown significantly in recent years. The need for new churches has never been greater. At the same time, the number of models and approaches are expanding. To address the unique opportunities of churches in this landscape, Exponential launched the Exponential Book Series in partnership with solid partners like Seedbed.

Books in this series seek to:

> Tell the reproducing church story;
> Celebrate the diversity of church-planting models and approaches;
> Highlight the pioneering practices of healthy, reproducing churches; and
> Equip kingdom-minded leaders with the tools they need in their journey of becoming reproducing church leaders.

Exponential exists to attract, inspire, and challenge kingdom-minded leaders to engage in a movement of high-impact, reproducing churches. We provide a national voice for this movement as we seek to champion multiplication.

The Exponential Book Series is part of a growing library of church multiplication resources that include Exponential conferences, learning communities, e-books, courses, webcasts, and audio training. The Exponential Book Series is an important element in our mission to foster church multipliers with thought leadership.

For more information, visit exponential.org.

OTHER BOOKS IN THE EXPONENTIAL SERIES

AND: The Gathered and Scattered Church by Hugh Halter and Matt Smay

Barefoot Church: Serving the Least in a Consumer Culture by Brandon Hatmaker

Discipleshift: Five Steps that Help Your Church to Make Disciples Who Make Disciples by Jim Putman and Bobby Harrington with Robert Coleman

Exponential: How You and Your Friends Can Start a Missional Church Movement by Dave Ferguson and Jon Ferguson

For the City: Proclaiming and Living Out the Gospel by Darrin Patrick and Matt Carter with Joel A. Lindsey

God Dreams: 12 Vision Templates for Finding and Focusing Your Church's Future by Will Mancini and Warren Bird

It's Personal: Surviving and Thriving on the Journey of Church Planting by Brian and Amy Bloye

Missional Moves: 15 Tectonic Shifts That Transform Churches, Communities, and the World by Rob Wegner and Jack Magruder

On the Verge: A Journey into the Apostolic Future of the Church by Alan Hirsch and Dave Ferguson

Planting Missional Churches: Your Guide to Starting Churches That Multiply (revised edition) by Ed Stetzer and Daniel Im

Sifted: Pursuing Growth Through Trials, Challenges, and Disappointments by Wayne Cordeiro with Francis Chan and Larry Osborne

Small Matters: How Churches and Parents Can Raise Up World-Changing Children by Greg Nettle and Jimmy Mellado

Transformation: Discipleship that Turns Lives, Churches and the World Upside Down by Bob Roberts Jr.

MORE TITLES FORTHCOMING! VISIT EXPONENTIAL.ORG/BOOKS FOR MORE INFORMATION.

CPSIA information can be obtained
at www.ICGtesting.com
Printed in the USA
LVHW080439120919
630786LV00007B/7/P